Busy Ant Maths

2nd EDITION

Pupil Book 4A

Series Editor: Peter Clarke

Authors: Elizabeth Jurgensen, Jeanette Mumford, Sandra Roberts

Contents

4-digit numbers (1)

Recognise the place value of each digit in a 4-digit number

Challenge 1

1 Write the 3-digit numbers shown by the Base 10.

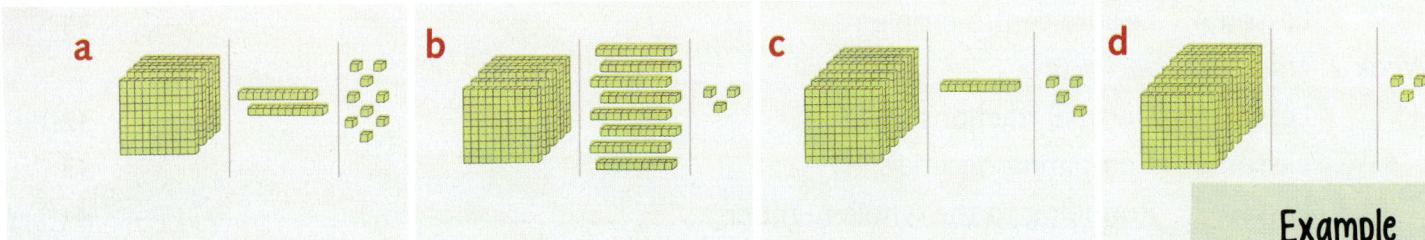

a

b

c

d

Example

753 = 700 + 50 + 3

2 Write the place value of each digit in these numbers.

a 538   b 413   c 681   d 390   e 759   f 827

Challenge 2

1 Write the place value of each digit in these numbers.

Example

4,736 = 4,000 + 700 + 30 + 6

a 1,295   b 2,861   c 2,649   d 3,804   e 3,382   f 4,741

2 These numbers have been decomposed into 1,000s, 100s, 10s and 1s. What is each number?

a 4,000 600 70 5   b 3,000 200 30 7

c 5,000 500 40 2   d 2,000 700 10 8

Challenge 3

1 What numbers have been decomposed into 1,000s, 100s, 10s and 1s?

I'm thinking of a number ...

a 20 400 1 5,000   b 9 3,000 10 600   c 4,000 30 200 6

2 I'm thinking of a number. The 1,000s digit is less than 4. The 100s digit is 4. The 10s digit is even. The 1s digit is 6. Find eight possible numbers.

4-digit numbers (2)

Recognise the place value of each digit in a 4-digit number

Challenge 1

Write the 4-digit numbers shown by the Base 10.

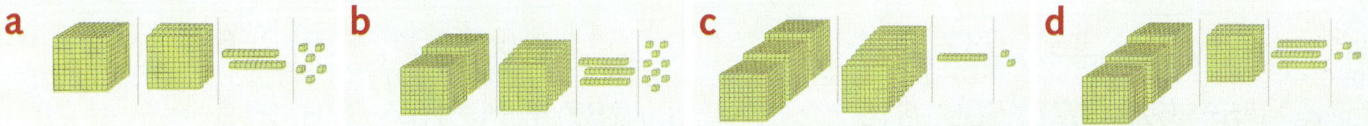

a   b   c   d

Challenge 2

1 Write the place value of each digit in these numbers.

> **Example**
>
> $1,352 = 1,000 + 300 + 50 + 2$

a 1,247   b 2,319   c 3,184   d 3,072   e 4,713

2 Write the numbers represented by the money.

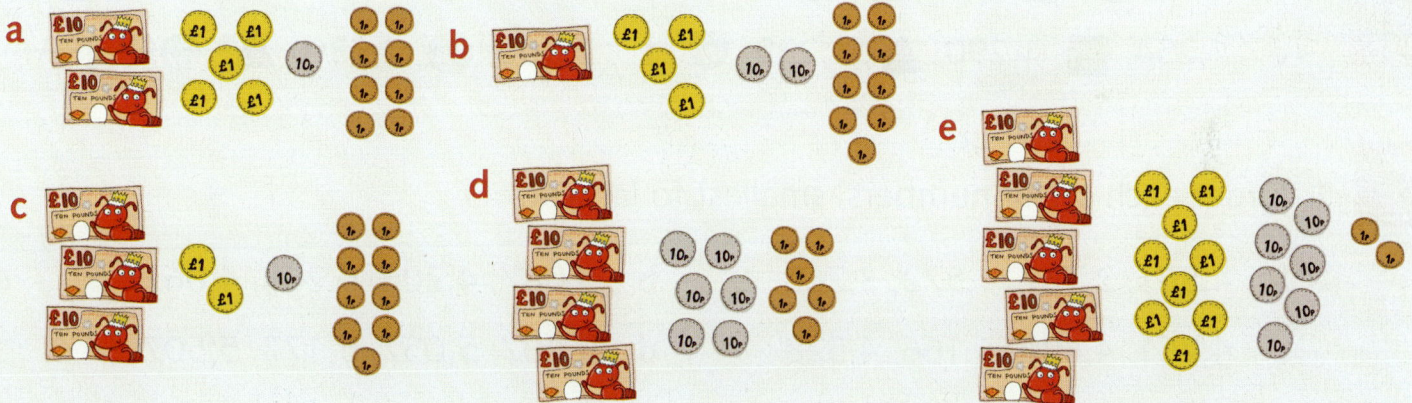

a   b

c   d   e

Challenge 3

1 I'm thinking of a number. What is it?

a It has one 1, eight 10s, nine 100s and five 1,000s.

b It has four 100s, nine 1,000s, six 1s and five 10s.

c It has eight 1,000s, three 1s, seven 100s and two 10s.

I'm thinking of a number ...

2 What would be a good way to estimate the number of leaves on a tree?

Ordering numbers beyond 1,000 (1)

Order and compare numbers beyond 1,000

Challenge 1

1 Order each set of numbers, smallest to largest.

   a 476, 286, 361, 582, 234   **b** 511, 151, 501, 155, 265

   c 755, 573, 675, 505, 615   **d** 287, 631, 167, 278, 218

   e 3,621, 1,467, 4,255, 2,854   **f** 2,765, 1,432, 3,362, 4,106

2 These numbers are in order. What could the missing numbers be?

   a 287, 295, ▲, 325, ▢, 361   **b** ▲, 388, ⬤, 415, ▲, 444

   c 623, ⬤, ▢, 698, △, △   **d** 1,000, ⬤, 1,087, ▢, 1,104, ▲

   e 1,254, ▢, 1,290, ▲, 1,299, ⬤ **f** 2,500, ⬤, 2,530, ▲, ⬤, 2,580

Challenge 2

1 Order each set of numbers, smallest to largest.

   a 4,861, 2,762, 1,572, 3,265   **b** 5,087, 4,206, 5,208, 4,062

   c 4,261, 4,482, 4,166, 4,528   **d** 5,207, 5,057, 5,177, 5,507

   e 4,012, 5,015, 5,011, 4,015   **f** 6,643, 6,628, 6,649, 6,612

2 a Use the number cards to make ten different 4-digit numbers.

   b Put the numbers in order, smallest to largest.

Challenge 3

1 Use the four number cards to make as many different 4-digit numbers as you can.
Organise your numbers in a systematic way to help.

2 Order your numbers in descending order.

2   3   5   6

1,000s more or less

Find 1,000 more or less than a given number

Challenge 1

1 Write the number that is 1,000 more than these numbers.

  a 365   **b** 276   **c** 831   **d** 3,671   **e** 2,995   **f** 4,329

2 Write the number that is 1,000 less than these numbers.

  a 3,825   **b** 3,199   **c** 4,794   **d** 4,067   **e** 4,326   **f** 5,439

Challenge 2

1 Write the number that is 2,000 more than these numbers.

  a 3,284   **b** 2,862   **c** 3,192   **d** 4,629   **e** 5,928   **f** 2,690

2 Write the number that is 2,000 less than these numbers.

  a 5,722   **b** 5,063   **c** 4,762   **d** 3,981   **e** 6,109   **f** 7,321

3 a Write six 4-digit numbers greater than 2,000.

  b On either side of your number, write the number that is 2,000 less and 2,000 more.

Example

2,877 ← 4,877 → 6,877

Challenge 3

1 Write the numbers that are 3,000 more and less than these numbers.

  a 6,341   **b** 3,842   **c** 5,999   **d** 4,025   **e** 5,827   **f** 6,297

2 a Write six 4-digit numbers greater than 4,000.

  b On either side of your number, write the number that is 4,000 less and 4,000 more.

Example

877 ← 4,877 → 8,877

Mental addition

Use mental methods for addition

Challenge 1

a 243 + 40	b 226 + 70	c 357 + 30	d 425 + 60
e 372 + 40	f 351 + 80	g 462 + 70	h 438 + 80
i 263 + 300	j 421 + 400	k 514 + 200	l 167 + 500
m 285 + 600	n 493 + 400	o 332 + 200	p 428 + 500

Challenge 2

Work out these calculations. Which can you do mentally?

a 479 + 80	b 424 + 500	c 682 + 70	d 516 + 80
e 372 + 600	f 173 + 700	g 945 + 90	h 286 + 800
i 140 + 38	j 190 + 62	k 270 + 58	l 320 + 67
m 470 + 173	n 510 + 197	o 560 + 172	p 590 + 165

Challenge 3

1 Work out these calculations. Which can you do mentally?

a 670 + 183	b 740 + 196	c 770 + 182
d 830 + 166	e 680 + 272	f 540 + 289
g 690 + 271	h 740 + 285	i 810 + 229
j 870 + 281	k 950 + 257	l 1,050 + 237
m 1,030 + 252	n 1,080 + 328	
o 1,250 + 426	p 1,370 + 538	

2,540 is a 4-digit multiple of 10.

2 Explain how to add mentally a 3-digit number and a 3- or 4-digit multiple of 10.

Mental subtraction

Use mental methods for subtraction

Challenge 1

a 176 – 40	b 253 – 30	c 247 – 40	d 283 – 60
e 235 – 60	f 213 – 40	g 346 – 50	h 362 – 80
i 365 – 200	j 428 – 200	k 481 – 300	l 537 – 300
m 529 – 400	n 631 – 200	o 617 – 400	p 682 – 300

Challenge 2

Work out these calculations. Which can you do mentally?

a 462 – 200	b 451 – 70	c 588 – 90	d 407 – 70
e 583 – 300	f 627 – 60	g 761 – 80	h 743 – 500
i 372 – 130	j 385 – 180	k 467 – 150	l 428 – 140
m 483 – 210	n 538 – 230	o 581 – 250	p 549 – 280

Challenge 3

1 Work out these calculations. Which can you do mentally?

a 537 – 250	b 586 – 310	c 693 – 270
d 715 – 240	e 783 – 260	f 801 – 180
g 846 – 270	h 956 – 360	i 984 – 330
j 927 – 310	k 968 – 370	l 1,007 – 220
m 1,067 – 250	n 1,038 – 180	
o 1,154 – 130	p 1,285 – 940	

540 is a 3-digit multiple of 10.

2 Explain how to subtract a 3-digit multiple of 10 from a 3- or 4-digit number.

1-step problems

Solve 1-step word problems in contexts

SCHOOL PLAY
Wednesday night

The children in Year 3 and Year 4 are taking part in a school play.

Challenge 1

1 On Wednesday, 68 tickets had been sold in advance but then 200 people arrived to buy tickets on the evening. How many people watched the play on Wednesday?

2 Year 4 always make the drinks to sell. They have prepared 150 cups of orange juice and 72 cups of apple juice. How many drinks have they made?

3 There were 224 seats put out for the play. 20 minutes before the play started, 70 were full. How many were still empty?

Challenge 2

1 140 seats had been put out in the hall, but 243 tickets had been sold. How many more seats did they need?

2 There were cookies for sale on Saturday evening. The stall started with 435 cookies and sold 240. How many were left?

3 On Friday evening 310 tickets were sold, on Saturday 168 tickets were sold. How many tickets were sold in total?

4 Thursday evening was when Year 3 and Year 4 parents came to see the play. 372 tickets had been sold. Year 3 parents had bought 190 of them. How many had Year 4 parents bought?

Challenge 3

1 Popcorn is always popular at the play. Year 3 made 665 bags to sell. After one night they had 365 bags left. How many had they sold?

2 Year 4 had prepared 486 cups of juice to sell one evening, but then the table collapsed and 190 were spilt. How many were left?

3 In total, 1,118 tickets were sold. On Thursday, 372 were sold. How many were sold on the other nights?

2-step problems

Solve 2-step word problems in contexts

SCHOOL PLAY
Saturday night

SCHOOL PLAY
Thursday night

The children in Year 3 and Year 4 are taking part in a school play.

Challenge 1

1 On Thursday Year 3 sold 45 tickets, on Friday they sold 80 tickets and on Saturday they sold 200 tickets. How many did they sell altogether?

2 The first part of the play lasted 63 minutes and the second part lasted 59 minutes. The interval was 30 minutes. How long did the whole play last, including the interval?

3 Year 4 made 300 cakes to sell. 48 were sold on Thursday and 170 on Friday. How many were left?

Challenge 2

1 On Thursday Year 4 sold 163 tickets, on Friday they sold 140 tickets and on Saturday they sold 300 tickets. How many did they sell altogether?

2 The popcorn was selling quickly. At 7:00 p.m. there were 300 packs. By 7:30 p.m. 137 had been sold. By 8:00 p.m. another 162 were sold. How many were left?

3 The school printed 430 programmes. On Thursday they sold 274, and 150 were sold the next night. How many were left?

4 After the play on Saturday, 340 seats had to be put away. 60 were taken back to the Year 3 classrooms and 73 to the Year 4 classrooms. How many were still in the hall?

Challenge 3

1 In the week before the play the children spent 320 minutes rehearsing. They did 125 minutes on Monday, 94 minutes on Tuesday and the rest on Wednesday. How long was Wednesday's rehearsal?

2 The school hopes to raise £450 from the play. They made £238 on Thursday and £170 on Friday. How much more do they need to reach their target?

3 The teachers helped with the preparations for the play. They spent 98 minutes decorating the hall, 260 minutes getting the stage ready and 380 minutes making the costumes. How long did their preparations take?

Symmetry in 2-D shapes

Identify lines of symmetry in 2-D shapes

You will need:
- mirror

Lines of symmetry	Road sign
None	
1	
More than 1	

Challenge 1

Place your mirror on each road sign to check for lines of symmetry. Copy and complete the table.

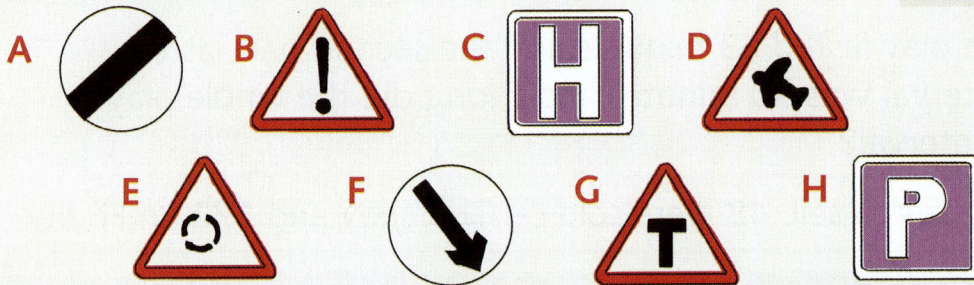

Example

Challenge 2

Use your mirror to test each shape. Write the letters of the 2-D shapes that:

1 Have no lines of symmetry.

2 Have 1 line of symmetry.

3 Have more than 1 line of symmetry.

Challenge 3

How many different symmetrical shapes can you make using six interlocking squares each time?

1 Draw each shape you make on squared paper.

2 Mark the line or lines of symmetry on each shape with a dotted red line.

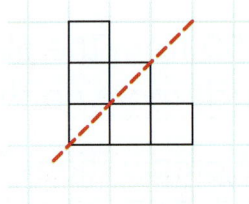

You will need:
- six interlocking squares in the same colour
- squared paper
- ruler
- red pencil

Reflecting 2-D shapes

Reflect 2-D shapes along a line of symmetry

You will need:
- mirror

Challenge 1

Place your mirror along the line of symmetry. Write the name of the shape you make.

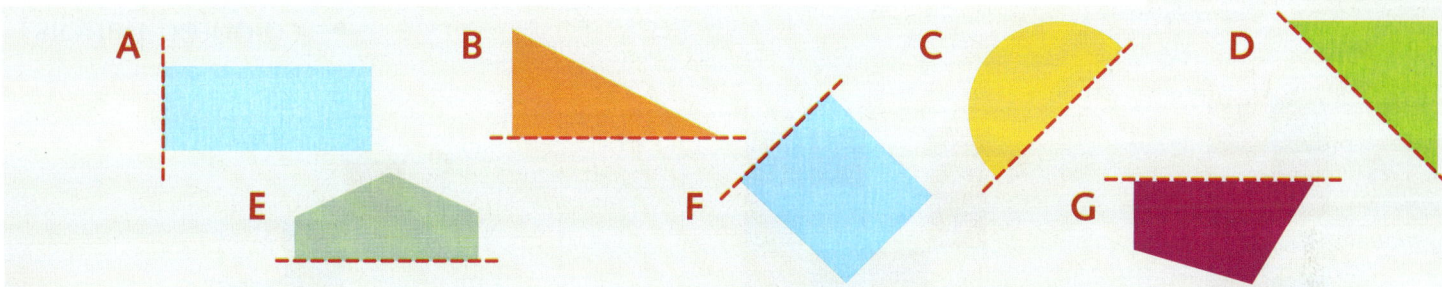

A   B   C   D

E   F   G

Challenge 2

1 These shapes are halves of shapes. For each shape, draw two possible whole shapes on squared dot paper.

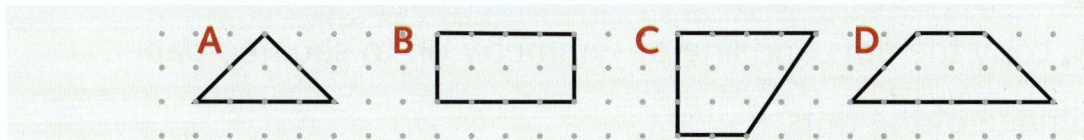

A   B   C   D

You will need:
- squared dot paper
- five interlocking square tiles
- ruler
- red pencil

2 Work with a partner.

   a Take five interlocking square tiles each and make a T-shape.

   b Find how many different symmetrical shapes you can make by joining both T-shapes together.

   c Record each shape you make on squared dot paper.

   d Mark the line or lines of symmetry with a dotted red line.

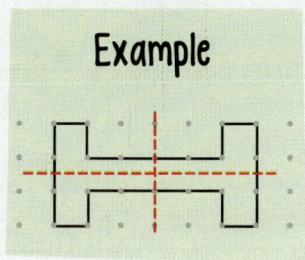

Example

Challenge 3

Imagine that the four shapes in Question 1 of Challenge 2 are all quarters of shapes.

   1 For each shape, find as many different whole shapes as you can.

   2 Record your shapes on squared dot paper and mark the lines of symmetry in red.

You will need:
- squared dot paper
- ruler
- red pencil

13

Completing symmetrical patterns

Complete simple symmetrical patterns using lines of symmetry

Challenge 1

1 Copy each pattern on to squared paper.

2 Colour the blank squares to make each pattern symmetrical.

You will need:
- squared paper
- ruler
- coloured pencils

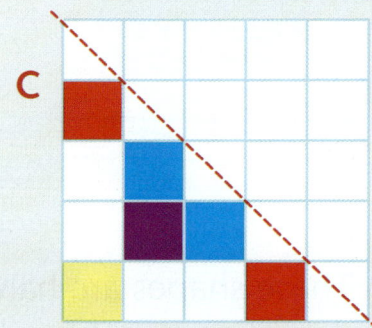

A   B   C

Challenge 2

1 For each grid below, copy the dots and line of symmetry on to squared paper.

2 Draw the reflected image of the dots:

a in 1 line of symmetry for grids **A–D**.

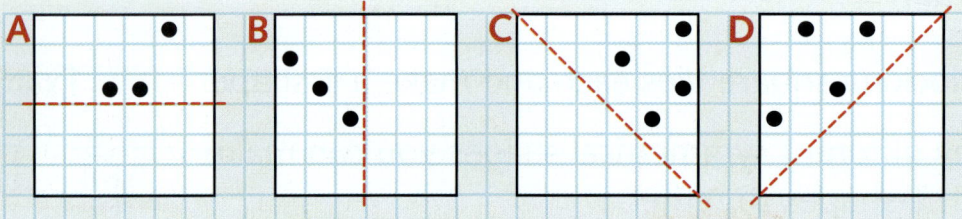

A   B   C   D

Example

1 line of symmetry

b in 2 lines of symmetry for grids **E–H**.

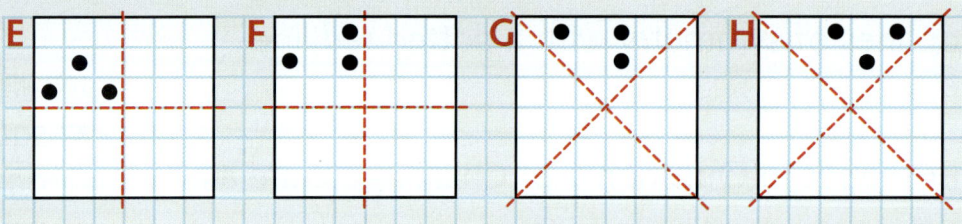

E   F   G   H

Example

2 lines of symmetry

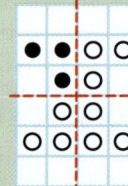

Challenge 3

Design a logo for a smartphone games app. Your logo should have 2 lines of symmetry.

Making repeating patterns

Make patterns by reflecting shapes in vertical lines of symmetry

Challenge 1

This pattern is made by reflecting a shape in vertical lines of symmetry.

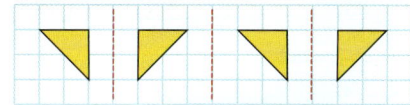

- Copy each shape below on to squared paper.

- Mark the lines of symmetry of each shape with dotted red lines.

- Reflect the shape to continue the pattern.

You will need:
- squared paper
- ruler
- red pencil
- coloured pencils

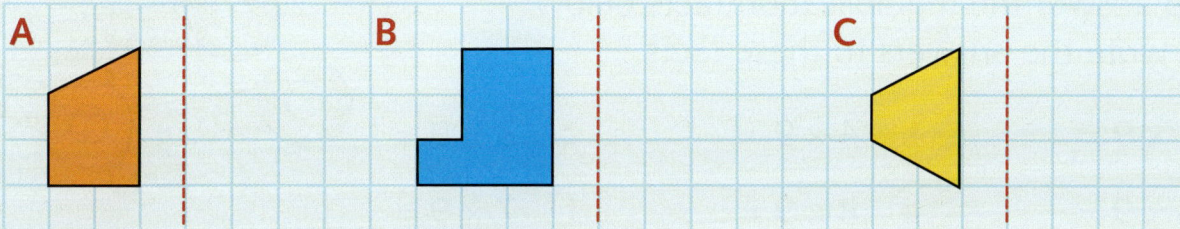

Challenge 2

- Copy each shape below on to squared paper.

- Mark the lines of symmetry of each shape with dotted red lines.

- Reflect the shape to continue the pattern.

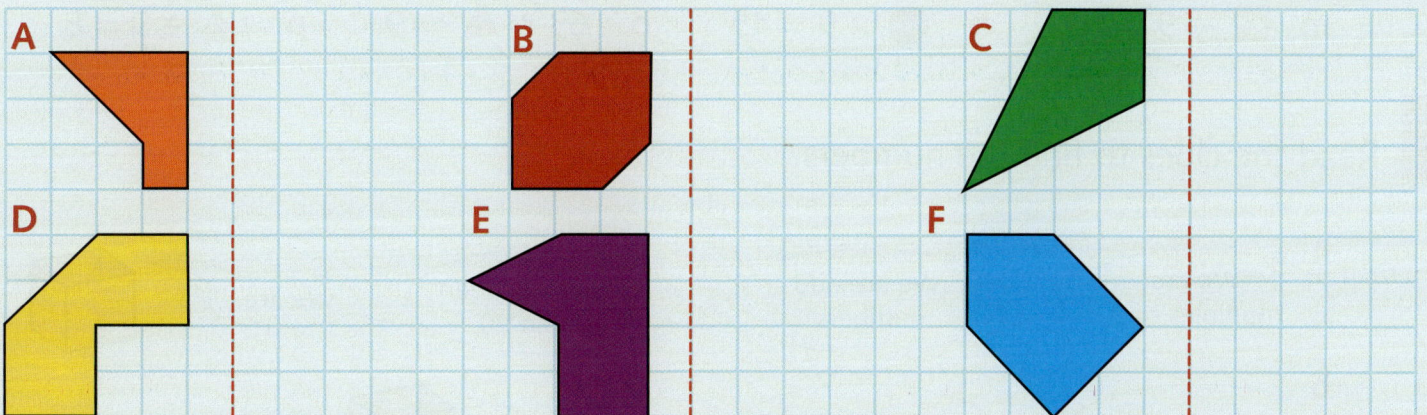

Challenge 3

Investigate the repeating patterns you can make by reflecting the following:

a   an 8-sided shape in vertical lines of symmetry

b   the complete pattern of your 8-sided shape in a horizontal line of symmetry

9 multiplication table

Recall the multiplication and division facts for the 9 multiplication table

Challenge 1

Some of the multiples of 9 have been written incorrectly in this number grid. Rewrite the number grid correctly in order, smallest to largest.

27	30	16	84
36	45	90	53
61	72	28	9

Challenge 2

1 Write down which of the key facts you would use to answer the multiplication facts below. Then write the answers to these facts.

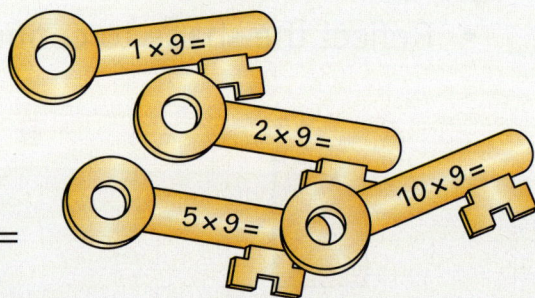

$1 \times 9 =$
$2 \times 9 =$
$10 \times 9 =$
$5 \times 9 =$

a $9 \times 9 =$
b $4 \times 9 =$
c $3 \times 9 =$

d $6 \times 9 =$
e $8 \times 9 =$
f $7 \times 9 =$

2 a $\blacksquare \times 9 = 27$
   b $6 \times \bigcirc = 72$
   c $9 \times \blacksquare = 63$
   d $\blacksquare \times 9 = 36$

   e $11 \times \blacktriangle = 99$
   f $108 = 9 \times \bigcirc$
   g $\blacktriangle \times 9 = 81$
   h $18 \div \blacksquare = 9$

   i $54 \div \bigcirc = 9$
   j $\blacktriangle \div 9 = 5$
   k $36 = \blacksquare \times 9$
   l $27 \div \triangle = 3$

   m $\blacksquare \div 9 = 10$
   n $\bullet \times 9 = 45$
   o $63 \div \blacktriangle = 9$
   p $\blacktriangle \div 9 = 8$

Challenge 3

Read the clues to find the numbers.

a We are multiples of 9. We are odd numbers. We are between 10 and 90. We are…

b I am a multiple of 4 and 9. I am between 20 and 40. I am…

c I am a multiple of 2, 8 and 9. I am an even number. I am less than 90 but greater than 60. I am…

Using the 10 multiplication table to learn the 9 multiplication table

Recall the multiplication and division facts for the 9 multiplication table

Challenge 1

1 Write the previous multiple of 9.

    a 18   **b** 45   **c** 36   **d** 81   **e** 90

2 Write the next multiple of 9.

    a 45   **b** 18   **c** 72   **d** 36   **e** 27

Challenge 2

1 Write the multiples of 9 that are two multiples of 9 more and less than these numbers.

    a 63   **b** 27   **c** 72   **d** 108   **e** 81   **f** 54

2 Write a multiplication fact for each number coming out of the machine.

a

1	5
6	4
2	3
8	7
9	10

×10

b

1	5
6	4
2	3
8	7
9	10

×9

Challenge 3

For each dartboard, multiply the number in the pink section by 9. Then multiply your answer by the number in the blue section.

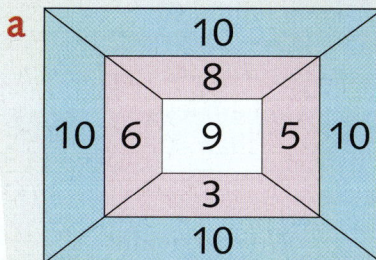

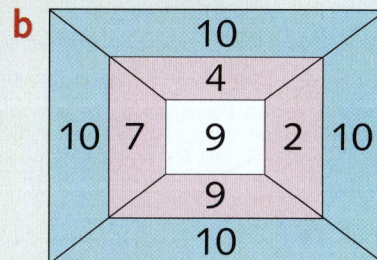

a

	10	
	8	
10 6	9	5 10
	3	
	10	

b

	10	
	4	
10 7	9	2 10
	9	
	10	

6 multiplication table

Recall the multiplication and division facts for the 6 multiplication table

Challenge 1

Write down which of the key facts you would use to answer the multiplication facts below. Then write the answers to these facts.

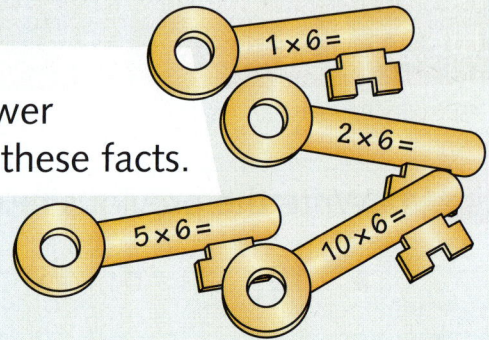

a $9 \times 6 =$ b $7 \times 6 =$ c $4 \times 6 =$

d $6 \times 6 =$ e $3 \times 6 =$ f $8 \times 6 =$

$1 \times 6 =$

$2 \times 6 =$

$5 \times 6 =$

$10 \times 6 =$

Challenge 2

1 One number in each trio is missing. Work out the missing number in each set of trios, then write two multiplication and two division facts for each.

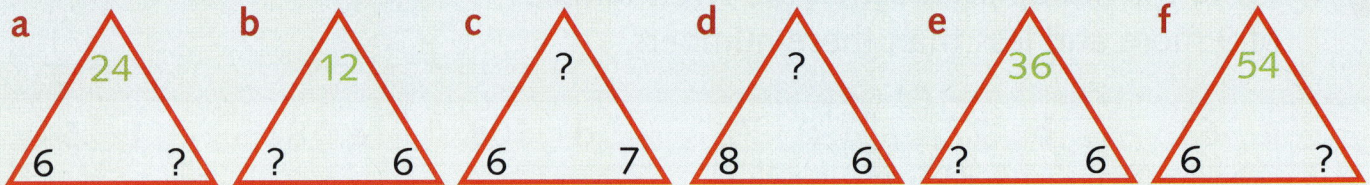

a 24 / 6 / ?   b 12 / ? / 6   c ? / 6 / 7   d ? / 8 / 6   e 36 / ? / 6   f 54 / 6 / ?

2 a $\blacksquare \times 6 = 30$ b $6 \times \triangle = 24$ c $6 \times \blacksquare = 36$ d $\bullet \times 6 = 42$

e $12 \times \triangle = 72$ f $6 = 6 \times \bullet$ g $48 \div \triangle = 6$ h $\blacksquare \div 6 = 3$

i $54 = \bullet \times 6$ j $12 \div \blacksquare = 2$ k $\blacksquare \div 6 = 11$ l $42 \div \bullet = 6$

Challenge 3

Read the clues to find the numbers.

a We are multiples of 6. We are less than 60. We have a 4 in the ones place. We are…

b I am a multiple of 3, 5 and 6. I am less than 40. I am an even number. I am…

c We are multiples of 3, 4 and 6. We are greater than 20. But we are less than 40. We are…

18

Using other multiplication tables to learn the 6 multiplication table

Recall the multiplication and division facts for the 6 multiplication table

Challenge 1

1 Copy and complete the number line for the 3 multiplication facts.

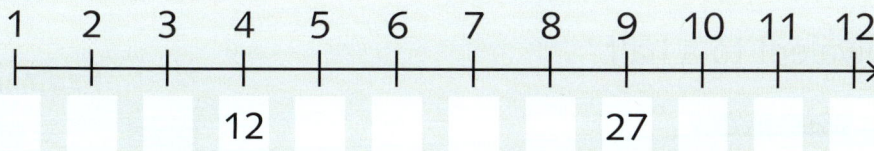

| 1 | 2 | 3 | 4 | 5 | 6 | 7 | 8 | 9 | 10 | 11 | 12 |

□ □ □ 12 □ □ □ □ 27 □ □ □

Hint

Use your completed number lines to recite the 3 and 6 multiplication and division facts, e.g.
$4 \times 3 = 12$,
$27 \div 3 = 9$,
$4 \times 6 = 24$,
$54 \div 6 = 9$.

2 Double the answers to the 3 multiplication facts to work out the answers to the 6 multiplication facts. Copy and complete the number line.

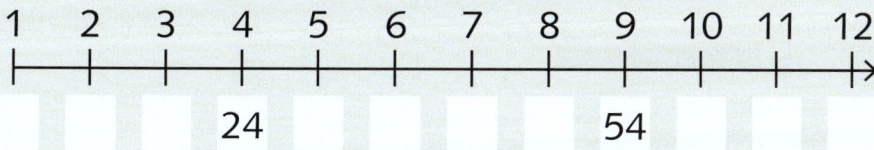

| 1 | 2 | 3 | 4 | 5 | 6 | 7 | 8 | 9 | 10 | 11 | 12 |

□ □ □ 24 □ □ □ □ 54 □ □ □

Challenge 2

Use the strategy shown to write the answer to the 6 multiplication calculations.

a 4×6 **b** 9×6 **c** 3×6 **d** 7×6

e 8×6 **f** 7×6 **g** 12×6 **h** 9×6

Example

6×6

(6×4) (6×2)

$24 + 12 = 36$

or

6×6

(6×5) (6×1)

$30 + 6 = 36$

Challenge 3

Write a multiplication fact for each number coming out of the machine.

a

40
90
30
80
70

×6

b

240
360
540
600
420

÷6

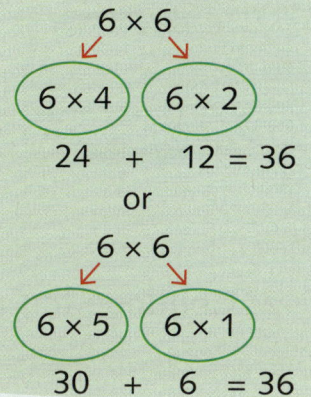

Equivalent fractions (1)

Recognise and show, using diagrams, families of common equivalent fractions

Example

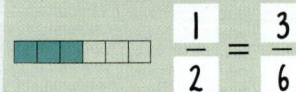

$$\frac{1}{2} = \frac{3}{6}$$

Challenge 1

Draw these diagrams and write the fraction equivalent to a half. Underneath write $\frac{1}{2} = \frac{}{}$

a 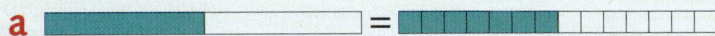   b

c   d

Challenge 2

1 Write the fractions equivalent to a half.

Example

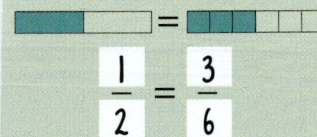

$$\frac{1}{2} = \frac{3}{6}$$

a 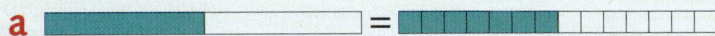 $\frac{}{} = \frac{}{}$

b 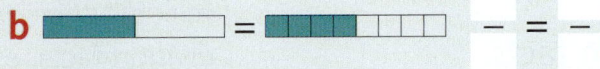 $\frac{}{} = \frac{}{}$

c 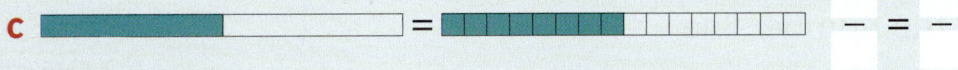 $\frac{}{} = \frac{}{}$

d 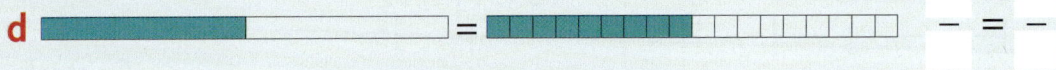 $\frac{}{} = \frac{}{}$

e 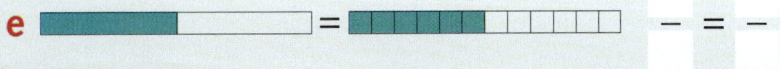 $\frac{}{} = \frac{}{}$

f 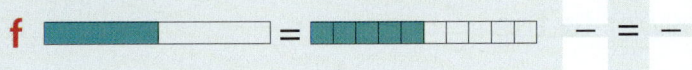 $\frac{}{} = \frac{}{}$

2 Continue this pattern: $\dfrac{1}{2} = \dfrac{2}{4} = \dfrac{}{6} =$

Challenge 3

1 Write in the fractions equivalent to a quarter.

a   b   c

2 Continue the pattern without the diagrams. Stop at 48ths.

3 What do you notice about all of the equivalent fractions?

Equivalent fractions (2)

Recognise and show, using diagrams, families of common equivalent fractions

Example

$$\frac{1}{4} = \frac{2}{8}$$

Challenge 1

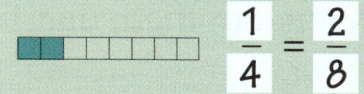

Draw these diagrams and write the fraction equivalent to a quarter. Underneath write $\frac{1}{4} = \frac{}{}$

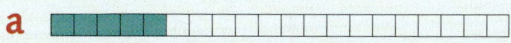

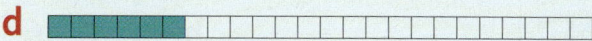

a

b

c

d

Challenge 2

1 Write the fractions equivalent to a quarter.

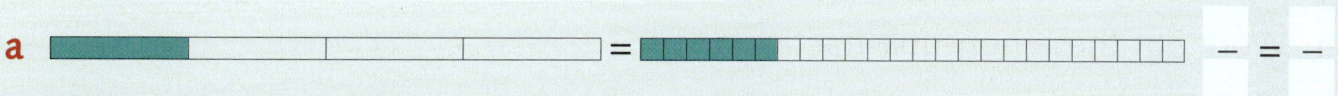

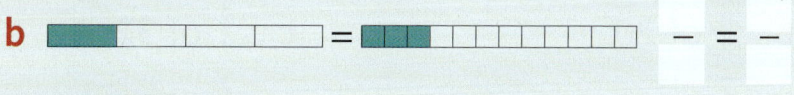

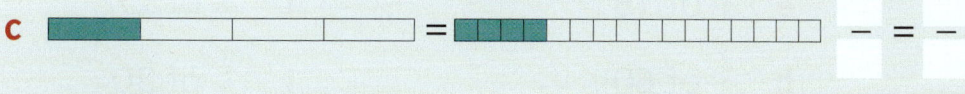

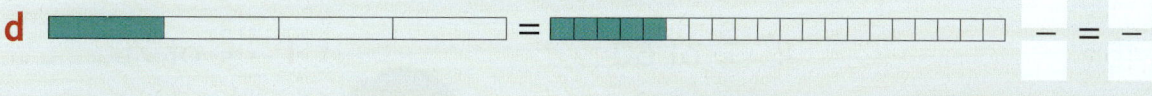

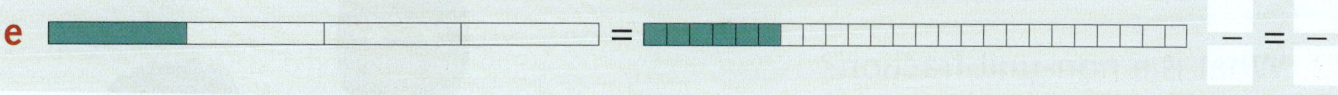

a $ = $ $\quad \frac{}{} = \frac{}{}$

b $ = $ $\quad \frac{}{} = \frac{}{}$

c $ = $ $\quad \frac{}{} = \frac{}{}$

d $ = $ $\quad \frac{}{} = \frac{}{}$

e $ = $ $\quad \frac{}{} = \frac{}{}$

2 Continue this pattern: $\dfrac{1}{4} = \dfrac{2}{8} = \dfrac{}{12} =$

Challenge 3

1 Write the fractions equivalent to three-quarters.

a $\quad$ b $\quad$ c

2 Continue this pattern: $\dfrac{3}{4} = \dfrac{6}{8} = \dfrac{}{12} =$

3 Explain the pattern.

Non-unit fractions (1)

Understand the relationship between non-unit fractions and multiplication and division

Challenge 1

Work out these unit fractions.

a $\frac{1}{2}$ of 22

b $\frac{1}{2}$ of 36

c $\frac{1}{2}$ of 80

d $\frac{1}{4}$ of 28

e $\frac{1}{4}$ of 48

f $\frac{1}{4}$ of 100

g $\frac{1}{3}$ of 24

h $\frac{1}{3}$ of 36

i $\frac{1}{3}$ of 42

j $\frac{1}{5}$ of 25

k $\frac{1}{5}$ of 35

l $\frac{1}{5}$ of 50

Challenge 2

1 Work out these non-unit fractions.

a $\frac{3}{4}$ of 12

b $\frac{3}{4}$ of 20

c $\frac{3}{4}$ of 32

d $\frac{3}{4}$ of 40

e $\frac{2}{3}$ of 18

f $\frac{2}{3}$ of 27

g $\frac{2}{3}$ of 39

h $\frac{2}{3}$ of 60

i $\frac{3}{5}$ of 30

j $\frac{3}{5}$ of 45

k $\frac{3}{5}$ of 60

l $\frac{3}{5}$ of 75

2 What is a non-unit fraction?

Challenge 3

1 Work out these non-unit fractions.

a $\frac{3}{4}$ of 60

b $\frac{2}{5}$ of 70

c $\frac{2}{3}$ of 90

d $\frac{3}{5}$ of 45

e $\frac{2}{6}$ of 54

f $\frac{4}{5}$ of 65

g $\frac{2}{5}$ of 70

h $\frac{4}{6}$ of 72

i $\frac{3}{5}$ of 65

j $\frac{5}{6}$ of 66

k $\frac{3}{6}$ of 48

l $\frac{4}{6}$ of 90

2 Explain how to find non-unit fractions of amounts.

Non-unit fractions (2)

Understand the relationship between non-unit fractions and multiplication and division

Challenge 1

Work out these non-unit fractions.

a $\frac{3}{4}$ of 12　　b $\frac{3}{4}$ of 24　　c $\frac{3}{4}$ of 40　　d $\frac{2}{3}$ of 15

e $\frac{2}{3}$ of 21　　f $\frac{2}{3}$ of 30　　g $\frac{3}{5}$ of 20　　h $\frac{3}{5}$ of 35

i $\frac{3}{5}$ of 40　　j $\frac{2}{6}$ of 18　　k $\frac{2}{6}$ of 30　　l $\frac{2}{6}$ of 42

Challenge 2

1 Work out these non-unit fractions.

a $\frac{2}{6}$ of 78　　b $\frac{2}{6}$ of 90　　c $\frac{5}{6}$ of 102　　d $\frac{4}{9}$ of 54

e $\frac{5}{9}$ of 81　　f $\frac{7}{9}$ of 36　　g $\frac{5}{8}$ of 96　　h $\frac{3}{8}$ of 112

i $\frac{7}{8}$ of 128　　j $\frac{4}{9}$ of 108　　k $\frac{3}{4}$ of 92　　l $\frac{4}{5}$ of 125

2 I have some counters. I halve them, then halve them again, then halve them again. Now there are 7 in each group. How many counters did I start with?

Challenge 3

1 Work out these non-unit fractions.

a $\frac{4}{6}$ of 138　　b $\frac{5}{7}$ of 133　　c $\frac{2}{8}$ of 128　　d $\frac{4}{9}$ of 135

e $\frac{3}{7}$ of 147　　f $\frac{6}{8}$ of 152　　g $\frac{5}{6}$ of 150　　h $\frac{7}{9}$ of 162

i $\frac{2}{7}$ of 168　　j $\frac{8}{8}$ of 176　　k $\frac{2}{3}$ of 198　　l $\frac{3}{4}$ of 184

2 I have some money. I spend half at the bookshop, a quarter at the supermarket and an eighth on sweets. I have £3.25 left. How much money did I have to start with?

Translating a 2-D shape

Recognise where a shape will be after a translation

You will need:
- squared dot paper
- ruler

Challenges 1, 2

Copy each shape **A–D** below on to squared dot paper. Translate each shape twice as follows:

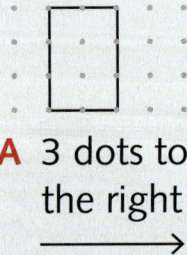

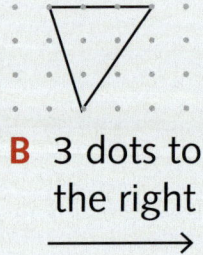

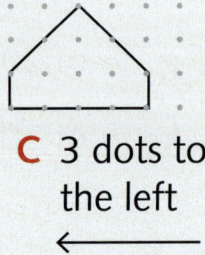

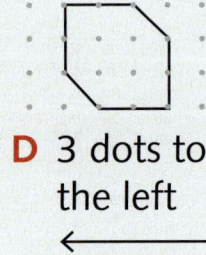

A 3 dots to the right →

B 3 dots to the right →

C 3 dots to the left ←

D 3 dots to the left ←

Example

3 dots to the right →

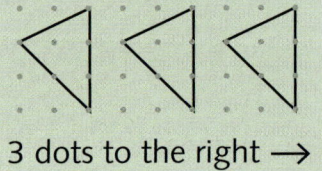

Challenges 2, 3

1 Translate each shape above twice as follows:

a shapes **A** and **B** – 3 dots up

b shapes **C** and **D** – 3 dots down

2 Write the instructions to translate the blue quadrilateral to the new positions **A–F**.
The first one (**A**) has been done for you.

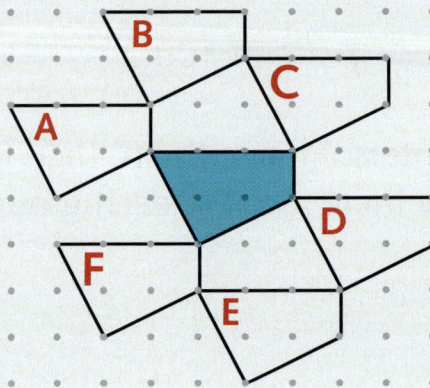

Example

A: 3 dots to the left then 1 dot up.

Challenge 3

Make patterns by translating the coloured shape:

- to the right and to the left
- up and down.

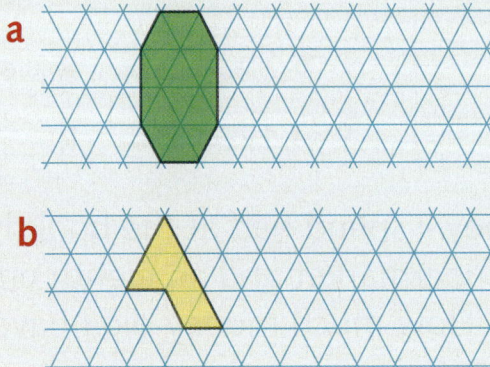

a

b

You will need:
- triangular grid paper
- coloured pencils
- ruler

Coordinates map

Use coordinates to describe the position of a point on a grid in the first quadrant

Example

Agent D is at the point (4, 3).

Challenges 1,2,3

The map shows where six secret agents are looking for a buried transmitter.

Write the coordinates for:

Agent A (,) Agent G (,)

Agent J (,) Agent M (,)

Agent Z (,)

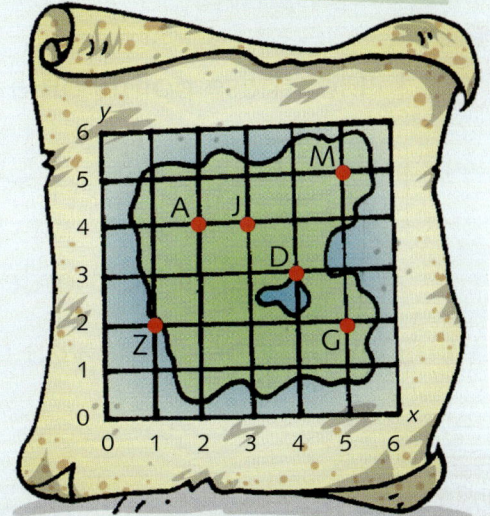

Challenge 2

1 Agent B is at a position between Agents G and M. Write two coordinates that show where he might be.

2 Agent B has this secret code on his laptop. Read the coordinates to find out where the transmitter is buried. Each line is a new word.

(5, 4) (5, 1) (4, 3)

(1, 4) (1, 1) (3, 1) (5, 1) (4, 4)

(1, 2) (3, 4) (5, 3) (3, 3)

(2, 1) (2, 3) (1, 1) (3, 1) (1, 3)

(3, 4) (5, 3) (3, 1) (1, 3)

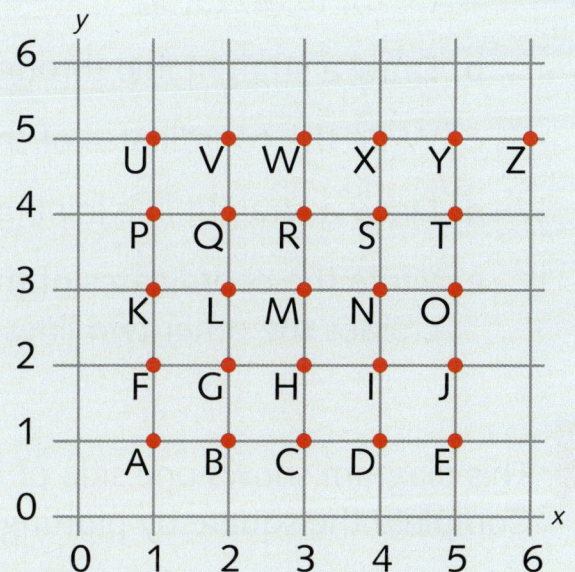

Challenge 3

Using Agent B's secret code:

• write your first name

• write in code where you would bury the transmitter, then ask a friend to read it.

25

Plotting the points

Plot specified points on a coordinate grid in the first quadrant

You will need:
- Resource 14: 6 × 6 coordinate grids
- ruler

Challenge 1

1 Plot these points on a 6 × 6 coordinate grid.

    a (1, 2), (6, 6), (1, 5)   **b** (2, 2), (2, 5), (6, 5), (6, 2)

2 Join the points in order with straight lines to make a 2-D shape.

3 Name the shape you make.

Example

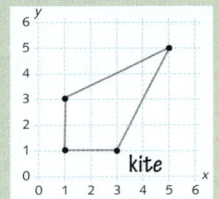

kite

Challenge 2

1 Copy the coordinate grid. The points show 3 vertices of a square. Plot and write the 4th vertex of the square.

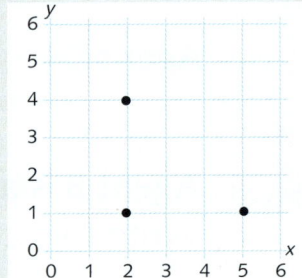

2 Copy the coordinate grid and the marked points.

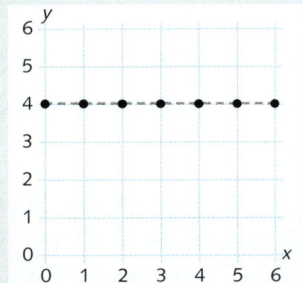

    a Plot these points on the same grid: (3, 0), (3, 1), (3, 2), (3, 3), (3, 4) (3, 5).

    b Draw a straight line through the points.

    c Write the coordinates of the point that the lines intersect.

    d Draw a straight line joining the points (0, 0) and (6, 6).

    e Write the coordinates of the points where the diagonal line crosses the other two lines.

Challenge 3

This diagram shows one side of a square.
Complete the square by plotting on the coordinate grid:

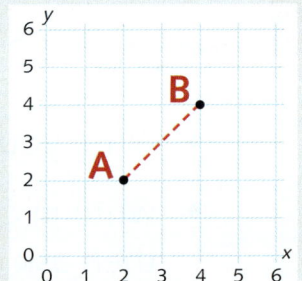

    a your first choice of vertices for points **C** and **D**

    b a 2nd set of vertices for points **C** and **D**.

Translations on a grid

Translate a shape on a coordinate grid in the first quadrant

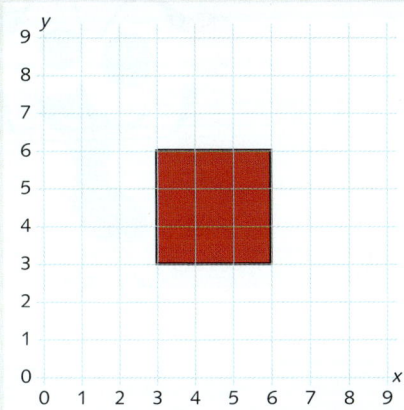

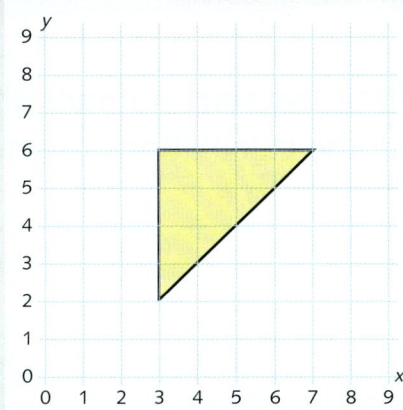

You will need:

- Resource 15: 9 × 9 coordinate grids
- ruler
- coloured pencil
- ICT tools (optional)

Challenges 1, 2

1 For each shape above:

 a copy it on to a 9 × 9 coordinate grid

 b translate the shape 1 square right, 1 square down.

2 Colour the shape in the overlap and name the shape.

Example

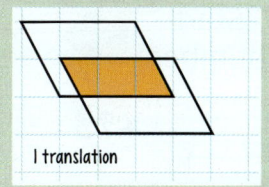

I translation

Challenge 2

Look at your answers to the Challenge 1, 2 activity. For each shape:

- Write the coordinates of the shape in the overlap.

- Translate the original shape 1 square left and 1 square up.

Example

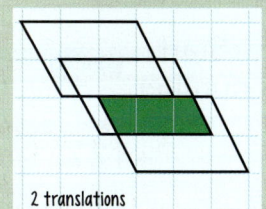

2 translations

Challenge 3

Copy the arrow on to a computer screen using ICT tools or on to a 9 × 9 coordinate grid. Translate the arrow as follows:

 a horizontally by adding 4 units to the x coordinate

 b vertically by adding 4 units to the y coordinate

 c diagonally by adding 4 units to the x and y coordinates.

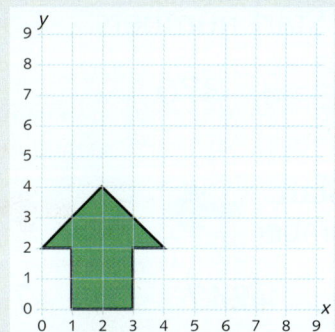

27

Addition chains

Use mental methods for addition

Copy the number chain, writing the start number at the beginning. Try to work out all the calculations mentally. Repeat for all five start numbers: **a** to **e**.

Challenge 1 Start numbers:

a 370   b 450   c 520   d 560   e 640

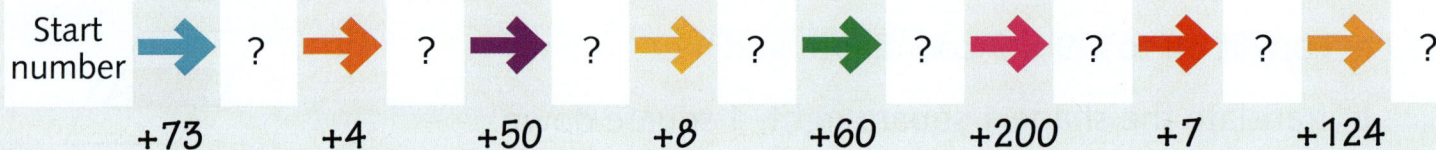

Start number →? +73 →? +4 →? +50 →? +8 →? +60 →? +200 →? +7 →? +124 →?

Challenge 2 Start numbers:

a 370   b 450   c 520   d 560   e 640

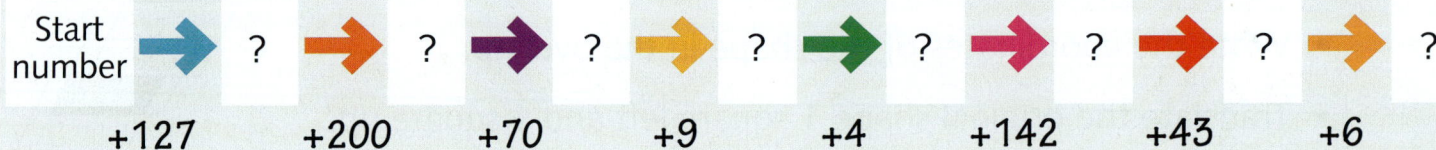

Start number →? +127 →? +200 →? +70 →? +9 →? +4 →? +142 →? +43 →? +6 →?

Challenge 3 Start numbers:

a 370   b 450   c 520   d 560   e 640

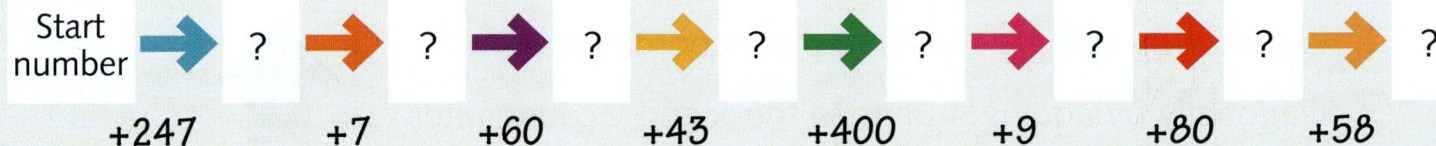

Start number →? +247 →? +7 →? +60 →? +43 →? +400 →? +9 →? +80 →? +58 →?

Written addition (I)

- Add numbers with 3 digits using the
  formal written method of columnar addition
- Estimate the answer to a calculation

Challenge 1

Work out the answer to each calculation using a written method for addition.

a	325 + 431	b	527 + 252
c	347 + 425	d	276 + 416
e	408 + 369	f	527 + 456
g	614 + 378	h	538 + 458
i	377 + 416	j	529 + 449

Challenge 2

Estimate an answer for each calculation, then work out the answer.

a	562 + 384	b	471 + 476
c	548 + 435	d	375 + 564
e	459 + 434	f	637 + 428
g	753 + 639	h	862 + 684
i	791 + 757	j	836 + 548

Challenge 3

Estimate an answer for each calculation, then work out the answer.

a	784 + 743	b	847 + 738	c	915 + 769
d	872 + 965	e	884 + 983	f	765 + 874
g	893 + 647	h	966 + 758	i	946 + 875
j	993 + 949	k	623 + 132 + 205	l	412 + 278 + 486

Decimal fractions

- Understand the place value of tenths
- Recognise and write decimal equivalents for tenths

Example

Fraction $\dfrac{3}{10}$ Decimal fraction   0·3

Challenge 1

Count the tenths and record them as a fraction and a decimal fraction.

a
b
c
d
e
f
g
h

Challenge 2

1 Write the decimal fraction that is of equal value to these fractions.

a $\dfrac{3}{10}$ b $\dfrac{8}{10}$ c $\dfrac{1}{10}$ d $\dfrac{4}{10}$ e $\dfrac{7}{10}$

f $\dfrac{9}{10}$ g $\dfrac{5}{10}$ h $\dfrac{2}{10}$ i $\dfrac{6}{10}$ j $\dfrac{10}{10}$

2 Write the next tenth.

a 0·5   b 0·8   c 0·3   d 0·1   e 1·4

f 1·7   g 1·5   h 2·7   i 2·1   j 3·6

Challenge 3

1 What is the decimal fraction that is of equal value to these mixed numbers?

a $1\dfrac{3}{10}$ b $1\dfrac{7}{10}$ c $2\dfrac{4}{10}$ d $2\dfrac{8}{10}$ e $3\dfrac{1}{10}$

f $3\dfrac{9}{10}$ g $4\dfrac{5}{10}$ h $4\dfrac{6}{10}$ i $5\dfrac{4}{10}$ j $5\dfrac{2}{10}$

2 Draw the number line and write in the tenths as fractions and decimal fractions.

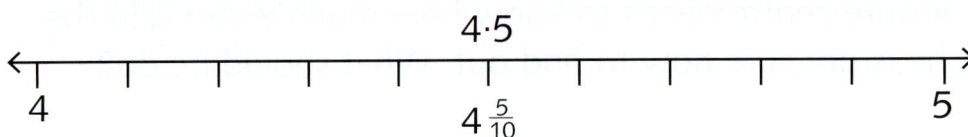

4·5

4          $4\dfrac{5}{10}$ 5

Comparing decimals (1)

Compare and order decimals with 1 decimal place

challenge 1

Count on in tenths for five numbers from these decimals.

a 0·7   b 1·3   c 2·5

d 3·2   e 3·8   f 4

g 4·1   h 4·7   i 5·5

Example

0·2, 0·3, 0·4, 0·5, 0·6, 0·7

challenge 2

1 Put these decimal numbers in order, smallest to largest.

a 1·7, 1·3, 1·8, 1·1, 1·9   b 2·3, 2·8, 2·1, 2·5, 2·6   c 3·7, 3·2, 3·8, 3·1, 3·9

d 4·5, 4·7, 4·3, 4·6, 4·1   e 5·2, 5·6, 5·9, 5·3, 5·1   f 6·6, 6·1, 6·9, 6·7, 6·5

g 7·2, 7·7, 7·9, 7·3, 7·1   h 5·3, 2·7, 1·9, 4·6, 3·7   i 3·5, 2·6, 3·1, 2·5, 3·8

2 Write the decimal numbers that are one tenth smaller and one tenth larger than these numbers.

a 2·7   b 3·1   c 4·8   d 4·5   e 5·7

f 2·9   g 8·2   h 9·7   i 10   j 12·5

challenge 3

1 Fill in the spaces with decimal numbers, keeping the numbers in order.

a ___, 7·7, ___, 8·3, ___, 9, ___, 9·5   b 8·1 ___, 8·5, ___, 8·9, ___, ___,

c 9, ___, ___, 9·6, ___, ___, 10·2, ___   d 10, ___, ___, 10·7, ___, ___, 11·3

2 Write the less than < or greater than > sign between these pairs of numbers.

a 2·5 ___ 2·7   b 1·6 ___ 1·9   c 2·8 ___ 2·1   d 2 ___ 2·6

e 5·5 ___ 3·5   f 7·8 ___ 8·7   g 9·3 ___ 9·1   h 12·5 ___ 11·4

Rounding to the whole number

Round decimals with 1 decimal place to the nearest whole number

Challenge 1

1 Look at the decimal number on the number line.
What number should it round to?

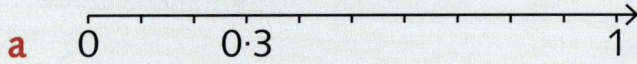

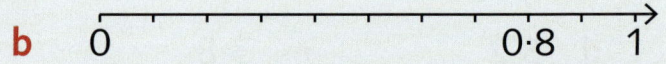

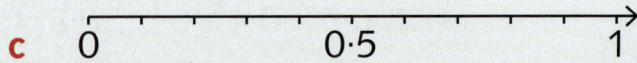

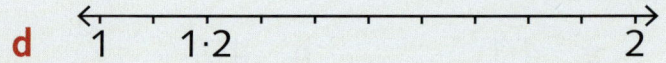

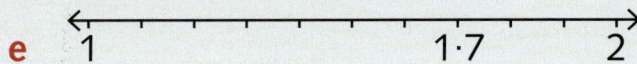

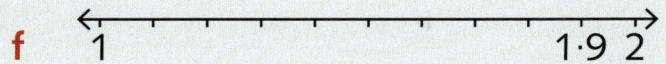

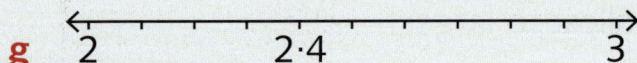

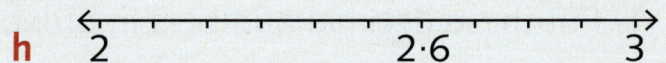

a   0   0·3   1

b   0   0·8   1

c   0   0·5   1

d   1   1·2   2

e   1   1·7   2

f   1   1·9 2

g   2   2·4   3

h   2   2·6   3

2 Draw a number line from 5 to 6. Fill in all the tenths.

   a Which tenths round to 5?   b Which tenths round to 6?

Challenge 2

1 Write the two whole numbers that each decimal comes between.

   a 2·6   b 1·3   c 3·7   d 5·9   e 6·5

   f 9·4   g 7·2   h 4·8   i 9·1   j 10·7

2 For each decimal number in Question 1, look at the tenths digit and decide whether the whole number should stay the same or round up. Circle the whole number the decimal rounds to.

Challenge 3

1 Write all nine decimal tenths that would round to each of these numbers.

   a 2   b 5   c 7   d 3   e 6

   f 10   g 13   h 15   i 16   j 24

2 Explain the rules for rounding tenths.

Sports day

Solve simple problems involving decimals to 1 place

Five children enter the long jump, the cross-country run and the 50 m sprint.

Long jump	
Name	Distance jumped
Helena	1·2 m
Robin	1·8 m
Maya	1·1 m
Fatima	0·9 m
Jake	1·5 m

Challenge 1

a Who jumped the furthest? How do you know?

b Put all the children in order of how far they jumped.

c Round all the children's distances to the nearest metre.

d Change all the distances to metres and fractions.

e Draw a number line like this and put all the children's distances on it.

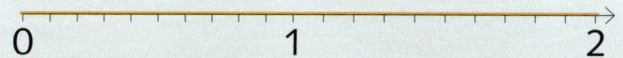

```
0               1               2
```

Challenge 2

a Put all the runners in order of how far they ran.

b Round all the runners' distances to the nearest km.

c Maya said to Helena, "I only ran 0·1 km further than you, but when we round our distance it seems I ran 1 km further than you." Is this fair?

d Change all the distances to kilometres and fractions.

Cross-country run	
Name	Distance run
Helena	3·4 km
Robin	2·9 km
Maya	3·5 km
Fatima	3·1 km
Jake	2·7 km

Challenge 3

a Put all the runners in order of their time.

b Round all the runners' times to the nearest second.

c Helena said to Maya, "When our times are rounded to the nearest second, your time improves and mine does not." Why is this? Is it fair?

50 m sprint	
Name	Time
Helena	12·4 seconds
Robin	14·5 seconds
Maya	12·6 seconds
Fatima	13·3 seconds
Jake	14·8 seconds

Recording mass using decimal notation

Record metric units for mass using decimals

Challenge 1

Write each mass in kilograms and grams.

Example
4,600 g = 4 kg 600 g

a   2,500 g   b   3,100 g   c   5,700 g   d   2,900 g

Challenge 2

1 Write the mass of each chicken in four different ways.

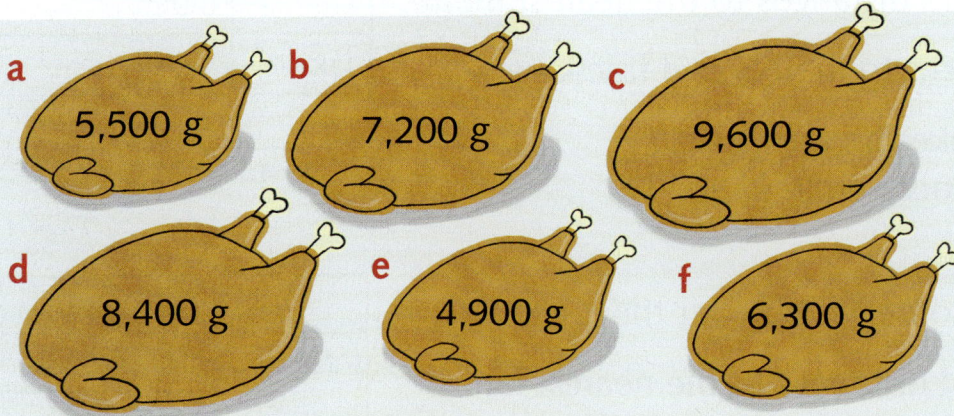

a 5,500 g
b 7,200 g
c 9,600 g
d 8,400 g
e 4,900 g
f 6,300 g

Example
$2,000 \text{ g} + 300 \text{ g}$ $2\frac{3}{10}$ kg
2,300 g
2 kg 300 g   2·3 kg

2 Write each mass in grams.

a   6·4 kg   b   8·5 kg   c   5·7 kg

d   13·1 kg   e   22·9 kg   f   17·6 kg

Example
7·2 kg = 7,000 g + 200 g
        = 7,200 g

3 Write the weights shown on these scales.

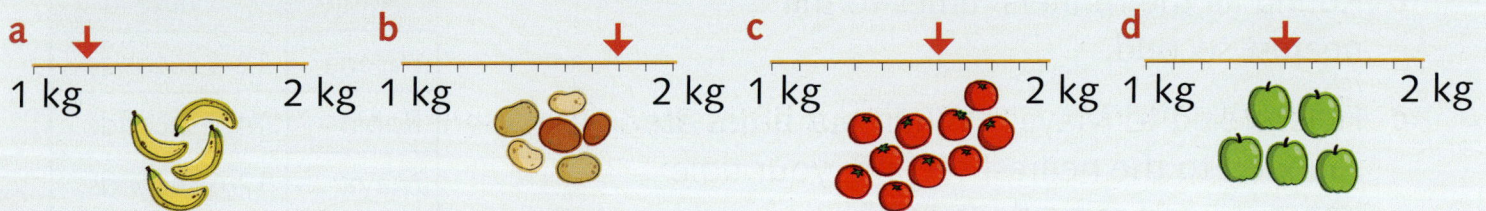

a
1 kg   2 kg

b
1 kg   2 kg

c
1 kg   2 kg

d
1 kg   2 kg

Challenge 3

Look at the scales in Challenge 2, Question 3. Find the approximate mass in grams of:

a   1 banana   b   1 potato   c   1 tomato   d   1 apple

36

Multiples of standard weights

Use multiplication to convert from larger to smaller units

Challenge 1

You have four standard weights.

Example

450 g = (2 × 200 g) + 50 g

Write the least number of weights you need to balance the mass of each kitten. You can use each weight more than once.

a 350 g   b 140 g   c 470 g   d 290 g

Challenge 2

You have six standard weights.
You can use each weight more than once to answer these questions.

Example

1 kg = 2 × 500 g

1   Balance 1 kg using: a 4 weights   b 5 weights   c 10 weights

2   Balance 500 g using: a 3 weights   b 5 weights   c 10 weights

3   Balance 100 g using: a 2 weights   b 4 weights   c 5 weights

4   Find four ways to balance 450 g using 50 g, 100 g and 200 g weights.

Challenge 3

1   How many different ways can you balance 750 g using 50 g, 100 g, 200 g and 500 g weights?

2   A baker has one 100 g weight and one 200 g weight. How can he use these weights to measure out 900 g of flour?

Square numbers

Recall square numbers to 12 × 12 and the related division facts

Challenge 1

Draw each of the square numbers in your book or on squared paper. Write the multiplication fact and related division fact for each.

a 2^2 b 3^2 c 4^2 d 5^2

e 6^2 f 7^2 g 8^2 h 9^2

Example

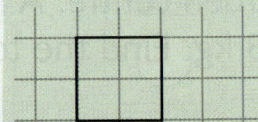

$2^2 = 2 \times 2 = 4$
$4 \div 2 = 2$

Challenge 2

Some of the square numbers are missing in this grid. Find the missing square numbers and write the multiplication and related division fact, starting with the smallest square number. The largest square number has been done for you.

⭐	25	⭐	64
⭐	⭐	81	⭐
16	⭐	⭐	1

start →

			$12 \times 12 = 144$ $144 \div 12 = 12$

Challenge 3

Work out the answers to these calculations about square numbers. Show your working.

Example
$6^2 + 5^2 = 36 + 25$
$= 61$

a $12^2 - 6^2 =$ b $9^2 + 7^2 =$ c $11^2 - 4^2 =$

d $6^2 \times 2^2 =$ e $8^2 \times 3^2 =$ f $12^2 + 8^2 =$

g $9^2 - 5^2 =$ h $7^2 - 2^2 =$ i $10^2 + 9^2 =$

7 multiplication table

Recall the multiplication and division facts for the 7 multiplication table

Challenge 1

1 Write the multiple of 7 that comes before each of these numbers.

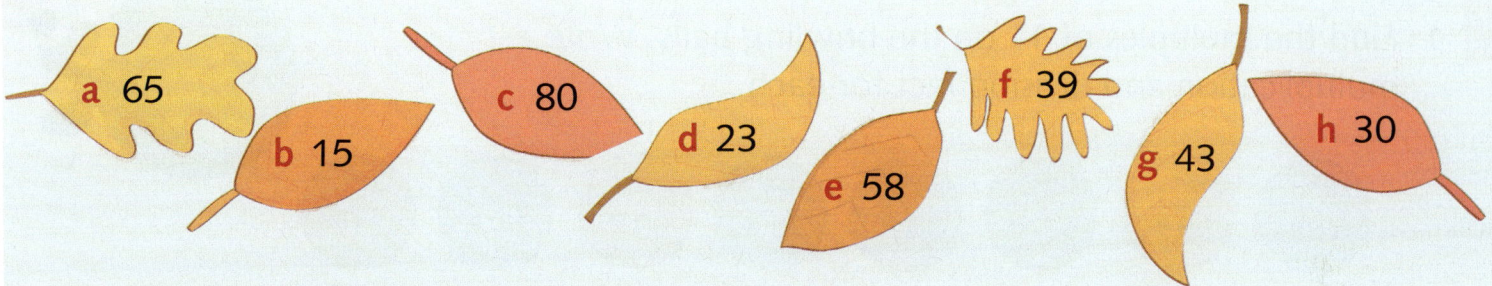

a 65
b 15
c 80
d 23
e 58
f 39
g 43
h 30

2 Write the multiples of 7 from 7 to 84 in order, smallest to largest.

Challenge 2

Find the missing number in each calculation.

a $\square \times 7 = 49$

b $7 \times 0 = \triangle$

c $7 \times \triangle = 63$

d $\triangle \times 7 = 35$

e $12 \times \bullet = 84$

f $7 = 7 \times \blacksquare$

g $\blacksquare \times 7 = 21$

h $28 \div \square = 7$

i $56 \div \bigcirc = 8$

j $\bigcirc \div 1 = 7$

k $42 = \triangle \times 7$

l $14 \div \square = 2$

m $\square \div 7 = 11$

n $\square \times 7 = 70$

o $49 \div \blacktriangle = 7$

Challenge 3

Read the clues to find each number.

a I am a multiple of 7. I am less than 40. I have a 1 in the ones place. I am…

b I am a multiple of 3, 6 and 7. I am between 40 and 60. I am an even number. I am…

c I am a multiple of 7. I am an odd number. My digits add to make a total of 8. I am…

41

Finding factors

- Recall the multiplication and division facts for the 11 and 12 multiplication tables
- Recognise and find factors of numbers to multiples up to 12 × 12

Challenge 1

1 Find the multiples of 11 on the bowling balls. Write a multiplication and division fact for each.

61 66 82 88 35 99 22 121

2 Find the multiples of 12. Write a multiplication and division fact for each.

36 60 64 144 92 132 72 86

Challenge 2

Find the factors of the number on each bowling ball from the numbers given on the skittles.

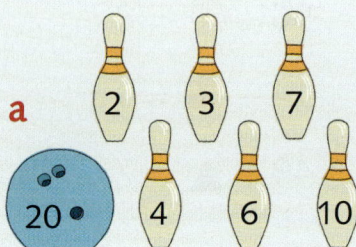

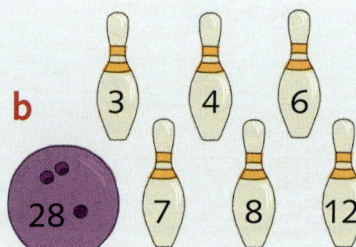

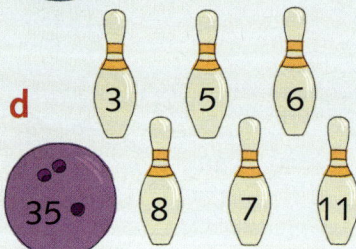

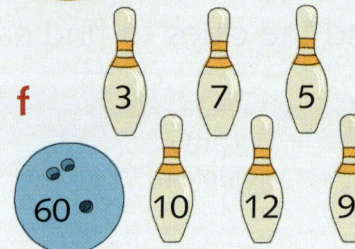

a 2 3 7
   20 4 6 10

b 3 4 6
   28 7 8 12

c 5 3 4
   18 6 9 8

d 3 5 6
   35 8 7 11

e 2 4 6
   30 5 3 9

f 3 7 5
   60 10 12 9

Challenge 3

Write all of the factors of these pairs of numbers. Find and circle the common factors of both numbers.

a 24, 16   b 36, 64   c 32, 48

Solving problems using multiples

Solve problems involving multiplication and division facts

Challenge 1

Sort the cards into four sets: multiples of 3, 8, 9 and 12.
Some of the numbers belong in more than one set.

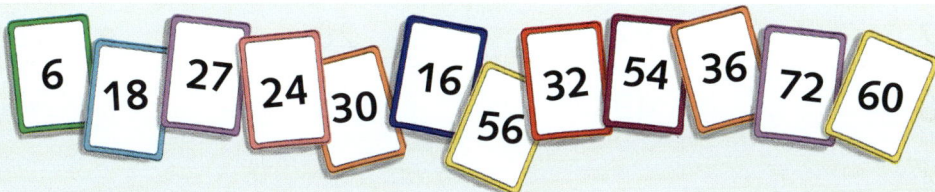

6   18   27   24   30   16   56   32   54   36   72   60

Challenge 2

Use the doubling strategy shown to write the
answer to each 12 multiplication calculation.

Example

5×12

5×6 5×6

30   +   30   = 60

a 4×12	b 10×12	c 3×12
d 7×12	e 6×12	f 9×12
g 12×12	h 8×12	i 11×12

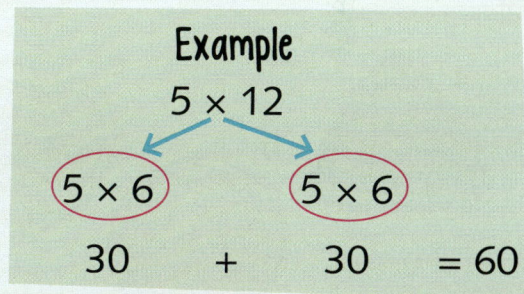

Challenge 3

Sort the multiples into the correct section in each Venn diagram.

a   24, 27, 36,
40, 32, 21,
15, 11

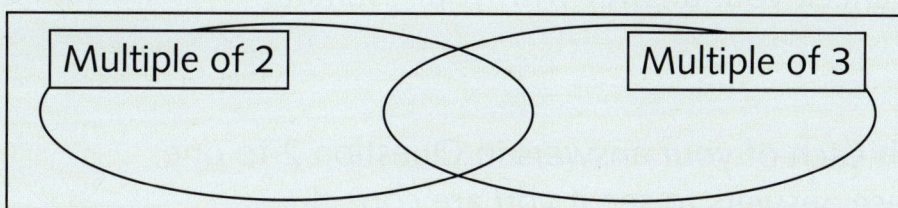

| Multiple of 2 | | Multiple of 3 |

b   16, 20, 32,
40, 25, 35,
44, 28

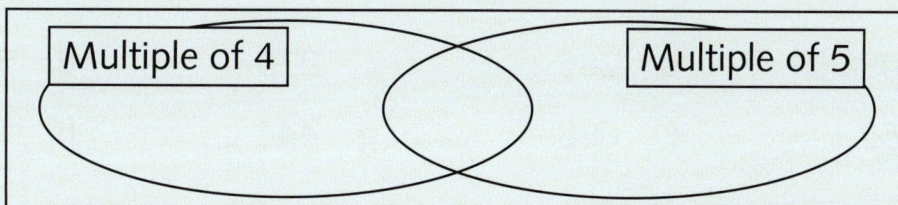

| Multiple of 4 | | Multiple of 5 |

c   12, 18, 22,
36, 56, 48,
24, 15

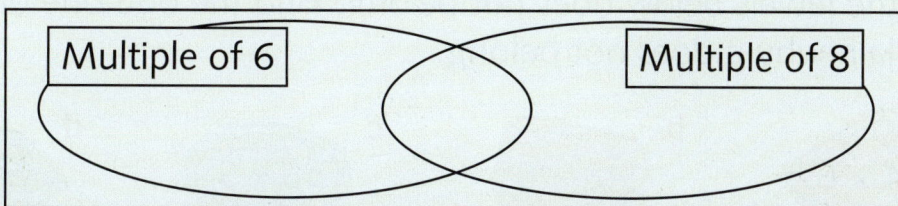

| Multiple of 6 | | Multiple of 8 |

Multiplication TO x O using partitioning

- Use partitioning to calculate multiplication of TO × O
- Estimate the answer to the calculation

Challenge 1

Write the multiples of 10 that come before and after these numbers.

a 73	b 37	c 87	d 26	e 62
f 11	g 48	h 49	i 55	j 94

Challenge 2

1 Write an approximate answer for each of these calculations.

a 57×5
b 74×6
c 63×4
d 86×8
e 48×3
f 39×7
g 27×9
h 87×6

2 For each of the calculations in Question 1, use partitioning to work out the answer. Then check your answer with your estimate.

Example

$63 \times 8 = (60 \times 8) + (3 \times 8)$
$= 480 + 24$
$= 504$

3 Match each of your answers in Question 2 to one of these answers to see if you are correct.

a 243	b 285	c 273	d 522
e 252	f 688	g 444	h 144

Challenge 3

One of the jewels below does not belong. Find the odd one out and explain why it does not belong.

a 64×6
b 48×8
c 58×3
d 96×4

Multiplication TO x O using partitioning and the grid method

- Use partitioning and the grid method to calculate multiplication of TO × O
- Estimate the answer to the calculation

Challenge 1

Partition these numbers into 10s and 1s.

Example
42 = 40 + 2

a
57
43
16
39

b
83
68
26
91

c
59
47
64
76

Challenge 2

1 Write an approximate answer for each of these calculations.

a 37 × 4   b 56 × 9   c 68 × 3   d 46 × 8   e 58 × 7   f 84 × 6

2 For each of these calculations, first make an estimate then use the grid method to work out the answer.

Example
63 × 8 → 60 × 8 = 480

×	60	3
8	480	24	= 504

a 47 × 5
b 53 × 5
c 38 × 4
d 32 × 4
e 26 × 4
f 91 × 8
g 64 × 3
h 74 × 3
i 85 × 3

Challenge 3

Some children used number cards and a 0–9 dice to make some calculations. They worked out the answers. Rahul forgot to write the number from the dice in each of his calculations. Can you work out which number he rolled?

a 43 × ☐ = 215   b 38 × ⬤ = 342   c 76 × ▲ = 532

d 57 × ▲ = 228   e 89 × ■ = 534   f 68 × ⬤ = 544

Multiplication TO x O using the expanded written method

- Use the expanded written method to calculate multiplication of TO × O
- Estimate the answer to the calculation

Challenge 1

Partition these numbers into 10s and 1s.

Example
87 = 80 + 7

a 45
b 38
c 63
d 56

e 74
f 82
g 27
h 94

Challenge 2

1 Write an approximate answer for each of these calculations.

a 56 × 4

b 86 × 4

c 38 × 3

d 69 × 7

e 54 × 9

f 28 × 8

g 79 × 5

h 47 × 6

2 For each of the calculations in Question 1, use the expanded written method to work out the answer. Then check your answer with your estimate.

Example

$$
\begin{array}{r}
6\ 3 \\
\times\quad 8 \\
\hline
2\ 4 \quad (3 \times 8) \\
4\ 8\ 0 \quad (60 \times 8) \\
\hline
5\ 0\ 4 \\
\end{array}
$$
1

Challenge 3

Choose three of your calculations from Challenge 2. Write a word problem to match.

Mental multiplications

- Recall multiplication facts
- Multiply together three numbers

Challenge 1

- Choose two number cards. Write a multiplication calculation and work out the answer.

- Repeat this for four more calculations. You must use each card at least once.

3 4 6 8
9 5
7 2

Challenge 2

a $3 \times 5 \times 8$ b $2 \times 8 \times 4$ c $6 \times 5 \times 7$ d $8 \times 9 \times 10$

e $7 \times 7 \times 0$ f $9 \times 6 \times 3$ g $6 \times 4 \times 9$ h $9 \times 7 \times 1$

i $9 \times 5 \times 3$ j $2 \times 9 \times 5$ k $6 \times 10 \times 7$ l $4 \times 6 \times 4$

Challenge 3

1
- Choose three number cards. Write a multiplication calculation and work out the answer.

- Repeat this for four more calculations. You must use each card at least once.

1 2 3 4 5 6 7 8 9 10

2 Which three consecutive 1-digit numbers multiply together to make these products?

a 120   b 24   c 504   d 60

Converting units of time

Convert between different units of time

Hint

s = second
or seconds

min = minute
or minutes

h = hour
or hours

Challenge 1

Copy and complete using numbers from the circles.

1 min = [ ] s   1 year = [ ] months

1 hour = [ ] min   1 year = [ ] weeks

1 day = [ ] h   1 year = [ ] days

1 week = [ ] days

24 60 365 7 12 60 52

Challenge 2

1 Write how many minutes there are in:

    a 4 h   **b** 6 h   **c** $8\frac{3}{4}$ h

Example

5 h = 5 × 60 min
     = 300 min

2 Write how many hours there are in:

    a 5 days   **b** 9 days   **c** 15 days

3 Write how many days there are in:

    a 7 weeks   **b** 12 weeks   **c** 52 weeks

4 Convert these times.

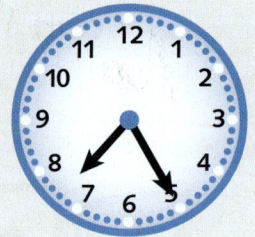

    a 50 h to days and hours   **b** 200 m to hours and minutes

    c 400 s to minutes and seconds   **d** 60 days to weeks and days

Challenge 3

1 For the months of April, May and June, find the combined number of:

    a days   **b** weeks

2 Write the age you are today in years, months and days.

Using 12-hour clocks

Convert time between analogue and digital 12-hour clocks

Example

20 minutes to 4 = 3:40

Challenges 1, 2

1 Write the digital time to match these 12-hour times.

a 12 minutes past 5   **b** 6 minutes past 8   **c** 27 minutes past 10

d 3 minutes to 11   **e** 14 minutes to 9   **f** 25 minutes to 1

2 Write the 12-hour times shown on these digital clocks.

a `4:23`   **b** `7:42`   **c** `10:09`

d `8:56`   **e** `2:25`   **f** `5:31`

Challenge 2

The airport clock shows the expected arrival time in London of the flight from Miami.

1 Write in digital form the flight's landing times for these days.

a Saturday: 8 minutes early   **b** Sunday: 14 minutes late

c Monday: 45 minutes late   **d** Tuesday: 24 minutes early

2 Write the 12-hour p.m. time the airport clock will show:

a in 3 hours' time   **b** 40 minutes later

c in $1\frac{1}{2}$ hours' time   **d** 75 minutes later

Example

In 1 hour's time
12:40 p.m.

Challenge 3

1 The table shows the landing times in London of the Miami flight for the rest of the week. Work out how early or late the landing time is for each day's flight.

Day	Landing time
Wednesday	11:17
Thursday	12:02
Friday	11:29

2 Look at the 12-hour digital clocks in Challenges 1, 2, Question 2. Write in digital form the time each clock showed $6\frac{1}{2}$ hours later.

Using 24-hour clocks

Convert time between analogue and digital 24-hour clocks

Challenges 1,2

1 Write the digital 24-hour clock time to match the a.m. time for each clock.

Example

6:00 a.m. = 06:00

a   **b**   **c**   **d**

2 Write the digital 24-hour clock time to match the p.m. time for each clock.

Example

6:00 p.m. = 18:00

a   **b**   **c**   **d**

Challenge 2

1 Write the digital 24-hour clock times for:

Example

5:15 a.m. = 05:15

   a   6:05 a.m.   **b**   half past 7 in the morning

   c   4:51 p.m.   **d**   25 minutes to 3 in the afternoon

   e   9:33 p.m.   **f**   17 minutes to 10 in the evening

2 Write the 12-hour a.m. or p.m. times for:

Example

18:00 = 6:00 p.m.

   a   14:45   **b**   22:10   **c**   07:57

   d   03:20   **e**   19:32   **f**   20:06

Challenge 3

Every 15 minutes a train leaves Milngavie Station for Glasgow. The first train after 10:00 a.m. leaves at 12 minutes past 10.

Write the times of all the trains between 10:00 a.m. and 2:00 p.m. in 24-hour clock times.

Changing times

Convert between different units of time to solve problems

Name	Time
Alex	266 s
Poppy	$4\frac{1}{2}$ min
Lenny	3 min 50 s
Yasmin	4 min 40 s

Challenge 1

The table shows how long it took four children to eat an apple.

  a Write the times for Poppy, Lenny and Yasmin in seconds.

  b Put the times in order, slowest to fastest.

Challenge 2

Name	Time
Chris	$3\frac{1}{4}$ h
Rob	3 h 35 min
Oscar	3.5 h
Scott	209 min

1 The table shows how long it took four boys to complete a cross-country race.

  a Write the times for Chris, Rob and Oscar in minutes.

  b Put the times in order, fastest to slowest.

2 A silver wedding anniversary marks 25 years of marriage. How many months is this?

3 The ship *Queen Mary 2* takes one week to sail across the Atlantic Ocean. Approximately how many hours is the voyage?

4 Use the information to work out the ages of four children.

- Archie: I am 2 years younger than Sarah.

- George: I am 12 months older than Archie.

- Emma: I am 3 years younger than Sarah and I'll be 10 next year.

Challenge 3

The table shows the times for sunrise and sunset in Aberdeen on 22 June, the longest day of the year, and on 22 December, the shortest day of the year.

1 For how many hours and minutes was the sun above the horizon on each day?

2 How many more hours of daylight does Aberdeen have on the longest day than on the shortest day?

Date	Sunrise	Sunset
22 June	04:20	22:15
22 December	06:50	15:35

Maths facts

Problem solving

The seven steps to solving word problems

1 Read the problem carefully.   2 What do you have to find?   3 What facts are given?
4 Which of the facts do you need?   5 Make a plan.
6 Carry out your plan to obtain your answer.   7 Check your answer.

Number and place value

1,000	2,000	3,000	4,000	5,000	6,000	7,000	8,000	9,000
100	200	300	400	500	600	700	800	900
10	20	30	40	50	60	70	80	90
1	2	3	4	5	6	7	8	9
0·1	0·2	0·3	0·4	0·5	0·6	0·7	0·8	0·9
0·01	0·02	0·03	0·04	0·05	0·06	0·07	0·08	0·09

Positive and negative numbers

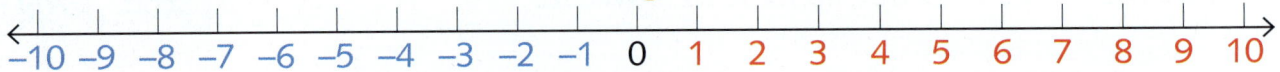

−10 −9 −8 −7 −6 −5 −4 −3 −2 −1 0 1 2 3 4 5 6 7 8 9 10

Addition and subtraction

Addition and subtraction facts to 10 and 20

+	0	1	2	3	4	5	6	7	8	9	10
0	0	1	2	3	4	5	6	7	8	9	10
1	1	2	3	4	5	6	7	8	9	10	11
2	2	3	4	5	6	7	8	9	10	11	12
3	3	4	5	6	7	8	9	10	11	12	13
4	4	5	6	7	8	9	10	11	12	13	14
5	5	6	7	8	9	10	11	12	13	14	15
6	6	7	8	9	10	11	12	13	14	15	16
7	7	8	9	10	11	12	13	14	15	16	17
8	8	9	10	11	12	13	14	15	16	17	18
9	9	10	11	12	13	14	15	16	17	18	19
10	10	11	12	13	14	15	16	17	18	19	20

+	11	12	13	14	15	16	17	18	19	20
0	11	12	13	14	15	16	17	18	19	20
1	12	13	14	15	16	17	18	19	20	
2	13	14	15	16	17	18	19	20		
3	14	15	16	17	18	19	20			
4	15	16	17	18	19	20				
5	16	17	18	19	20					
6	17	18	19	20						
7	18	19	20							
8	19	20								
9	20									

Multiples of 10 and 100 addition and subtraction facts

+	0	10	20	30	40	50	60	70	80	90	100
0	0	10	20	30	40	50	60	70	80	90	100
10	10	20	30	40	50	60	70	80	90	100	110
20	20	30	40	50	60	70	80	90	100	110	120
30	30	40	50	60	70	80	90	100	110	120	130
40	40	50	60	70	80	90	100	110	120	130	140
50	50	60	70	80	90	100	110	120	130	140	150
60	60	70	80	90	100	110	120	130	140	150	160
70	70	80	90	100	110	120	130	140	150	160	170
80	80	90	100	110	120	130	140	150	160	170	180
90	90	100	110	120	130	140	150	160	170	180	190
100	100	110	120	130	140	150	160	170	180	190	200

+	0	100	200	300	400	500	600	700	800	900	1,000
0	0	100	200	300	400	500	600	700	800	900	1,000
100	100	200	300	400	500	600	700	800	900	1,000	1,100
200	200	300	400	500	600	700	800	900	1,000	1,100	1,200
300	300	400	500	600	700	800	900	1,000	1,100	1,200	1,300
400	400	500	600	700	800	900	1,000	1,100	1,200	1,300	1,400
500	500	600	700	800	900	1,000	1,100	1,200	1,300	1,400	1,500
600	600	700	800	900	1,000	1,100	1,200	1,300	1,400	1,500	1,600
700	700	800	900	1,000	1,100	1,200	1,300	1,400	1,500	1,600	1,700
800	800	900	1,000	1,100	1,200	1,300	1,400	1,500	1,600	1,700	1,800
900	900	1,000	1,100	1,200	1,300	1,400	1,500	1,600	1,700	1,800	1,900
1,000	1,000	1,100	1,200	1,300	1,400	1,500	1,600	1,700	1,800	1,900	2,000

Written methods – addition

Example: 2,456 + 5,378

Expanded written method

```
   2 4 5 6
 + 5 3 7 8
   ─────────
       1 4
     1 2 0
     7 0 0
   7 0 0 0
   ─────────
   7 8 3 4
```

Formal written method

```
   2 4 5 6
 + 5 3 7 8
   ─────────
   7 8 3 4
     1 1
```

Written methods – subtraction

Example: 6,418 – 2,546

Expanded written method

```
    5,000    1,300    110
    6,000     400     10    8
  − 2,000     500     40    6
    ─────    ─────    ───   ──
    3,000     800     70    2
```

3,000 + 800 + 70 + 2 = 3,872

Formal written method

```
     5  13  11
   6  4  1  8
 − 2  5  4  6
   ───────────
   3  8  7  2
```

Multiplication and division

Multiplication and division facts

×	1	2	3	4	5	6	7	8	9	10	11	12
1	1	2	3	4	5	6	7	8	9	10	11	12
2	2	4	6	8	10	12	14	16	18	20	22	24
3	3	6	9	12	15	18	21	24	27	30	33	36
4	4	8	12	16	20	24	28	32	36	40	44	48
5	5	10	15	20	25	30	35	40	45	50	55	60
6	6	12	18	24	30	36	42	48	54	60	66	72
7	7	14	21	28	35	42	49	56	63	70	77	84
8	8	16	24	32	40	48	56	64	72	80	88	96
9	9	18	27	36	45	54	63	72	81	90	99	108
10	10	20	30	40	50	60	70	80	90	100	110	120
11	11	22	33	44	55	66	77	88	99	110	121	132
12	12	24	36	48	60	72	84	96	108	120	132	144

×	10	20	30	40	50	60	70	80	90	100	110	120
1	10	20	30	40	50	60	70	80	90	100	110	120
2	20	40	60	80	100	120	140	160	180	200	220	240
3	30	60	90	120	150	180	210	240	270	300	330	360
4	40	80	120	160	200	240	280	320	360	400	440	480
5	50	100	150	200	250	300	350	400	450	500	550	600
6	60	120	180	240	300	360	420	480	540	600	660	720
7	70	140	210	280	350	420	490	560	630	700	770	840
8	80	160	240	320	400	480	560	640	720	800	880	960
9	90	180	270	360	450	540	630	720	810	900	990	1,080
10	100	200	300	400	500	600	700	800	900	1,000	1,100	1,200
11	110	220	330	440	550	660	770	880	990	1,100	1,210	1,320
12	120	240	360	480	600	720	840	960	1,080	1,200	1,320	1,440

Written methods – multiplication

Example: 356 × 7

Partitioning

356 × 7 = (300 × 7) + (50 × 7) + (6 × 7)
= 2,100 + 350 + 42
= 2,492

Grid method

×	300	50	6
7	2,100	350	42

= 2,492

Expanded written method

```
     3 5 6
   ×     7
   ────────
      4 2   (6 × 7)
    3 5 0   (50 × 7)
  2 1 0 0   (300 × 7)
  ──────────
  2 4 9 2
```

Formal written method

```
     3 5 6
   ×     7
   ────────
   2 4 9 2
     3 4
```

```
       3   4
     3 5 6
   ×     7
   ────────
   2 4 9 2
```

> You can also write the regrouped value like this.

Written methods – division

Example: 486 ÷ 9

Partitioning

486
450   36

486 ÷ 9 = (450 ÷ 9) + (36 ÷ 9)
= 50 + 4
= 54

450 ÷ 9
36 ÷ 9

50 + 4 = 54

Expanded written method

```
           5 4
       9) 4 8 6
        − 4 5 0   (50 × 9)
          ─────
            3 6
          − 3 6   (4 × 9)
          ─────
              0
```

Formal written method

```
           5 4
       9) 4 ⁴8 ³6
```

> You can also include the related multiplication facts.

Fractions and decimals

$$\frac{1}{100} = 0\cdot01 \qquad \frac{25}{100} = \frac{1}{4} = 0\cdot25$$

$$\frac{2}{100} = \frac{1}{50} = 0\cdot02 \qquad \frac{50}{100} = \frac{1}{2} = 0\cdot5$$

$$\frac{5}{100} = \frac{1}{20} = 0\cdot05 \qquad \frac{75}{100} = \frac{3}{4} = 0\cdot75$$

$$\frac{10}{100} = \frac{1}{10} = 0\cdot1 \qquad \frac{100}{100} = 1$$

$$\frac{20}{100} = \frac{1}{5} = 0\cdot2$$

30 days has September, April, June and November. All the rest have 31, except February alone which has 28 days clear and 29 in each leap year.

Measurement

Length

1 kilometre (km) = 1,000 metres (m)

0·1 km = 100 m

1 m = 100 centimetres (cm) = 1,000 millimetres (mm)

0·1 m = 10 cm = 100 mm

1 cm = 10 mm

0·1 cm = 1 mm

Mass

1 kilogram (kg) = 1,000 grams (g)

0·1 kg = 100g

0.01 kg = 10 g

Capacity

1 litre (*l*) = 1,000 millilitres (ml)

0·1 *l* = 100 ml

0·01 *l* = 10 ml

Time

1 year = 12 months

= 365 days

= 366 days (leap year)

1 week = 7 days

1 day = 24 hours

1 hour = 60 minutes

1 minute = 60 seconds

12-hour clock

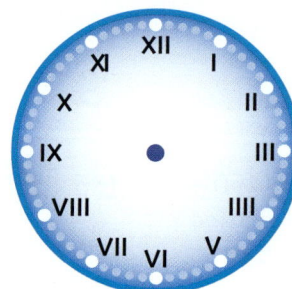

24-hour clock

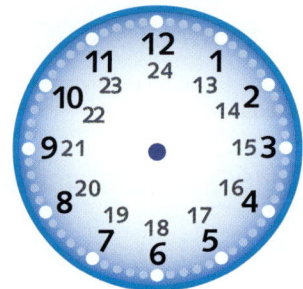

William Collins' dream of knowledge for all began with the publication of his first book in 1819.

A self-educated mill worker, he not only enriched millions of lives, but also founded a flourishing publishing house. Today, staying true to this spirit, Collins books are packed with inspiration, innovation and practical expertise.

They place you at the centre of a world of possibility and give you exactly what you need to explore it.

Collins. Freedom to teach.

Published by Collins

An imprint of HarperCollins*Publishers*
The News Building, 1 London Bridge Street, London, SE1 9GF, UK

HarperCollins*Publishers*
Macken House, 39/40 Mayor Street Upper, Dublin 1, D01 C9W8, Ireland

Browse the complete Collins catalogue at
collins.co.uk

British Library Cataloguing-in-Publication Data

A catalogue record for this publication is available from the British Library.

Series editor: Peter Clarke
Cover design and artwork: Amparo Barrera
Internal design concept: Amparo Barrera
Designer: Niki Merrett
Typesetter: David Jimenez
Illustrators: Louise Forshaw, Steven Woods, Gwyneth Williamson and Eva Sassin
Printed and bound in Great Britain by Martins the Printers

Busy Ant Maths 2nd edition components are compatible with the 1st edition of Busy Ant Maths.

Properties of shape

2-D shapes

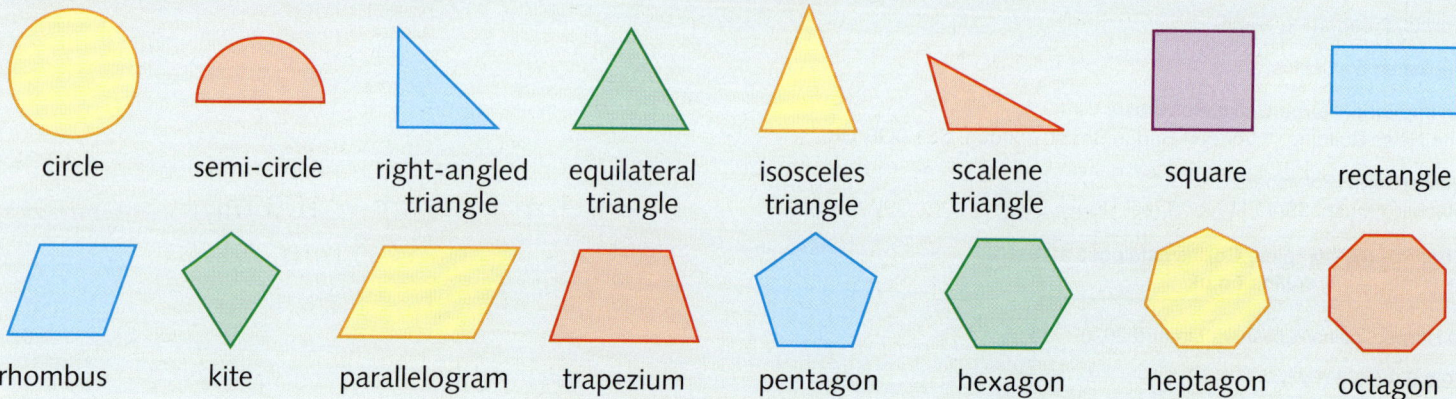

circle • semi-circle • right-angled triangle • equilateral triangle • isosceles triangle • scalene triangle • square • rectangle

rhombus • kite • parallelogram • trapezium • pentagon • hexagon • heptagon • octagon

3-D shapes

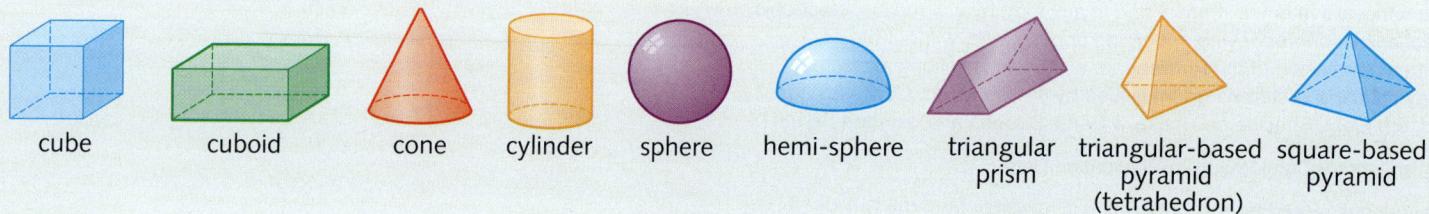

cube • cuboid • cone • cylinder • sphere • hemi-sphere • triangular prism • triangular-based pyramid (tetrahedron) • square-based pyramid

Angles

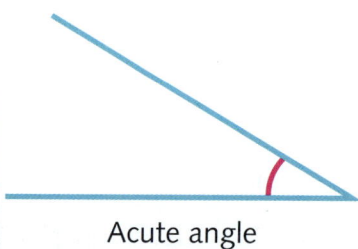

Acute angle

Right angle

Obtuse angle

Position and direction

Coordinates

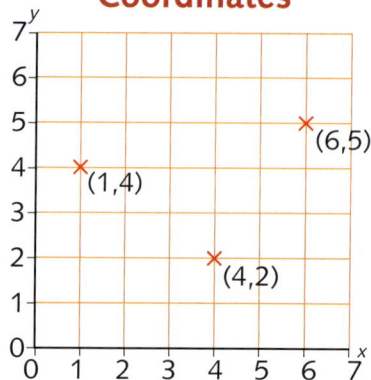

Translation

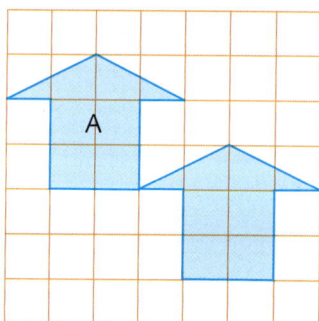

Shape A has been translated 3 squares to the right and 2 squares down.

Reflection

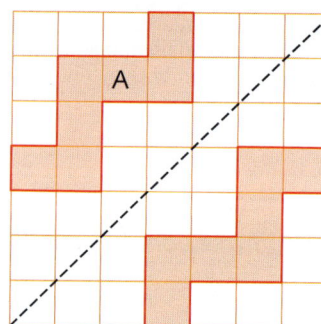

Shape A has been reflected along the diagonal line of symmetry.